SAGE was founded in 1965 by Sara Miller McCune to support the dissemination of usable knowledge by publishing innovative and high-quality research and teaching content. Today, we publish over 900 journals, including those of more than 400 learned societies, more than 800 new books per year, and a growing range of library products including archives, data, case studies, reports, and video. SAGE remains majority-owned by our founder, and after Sara's lifetime will become owned by a charitable trust that secures our continued independence.

Los Angeles | London | New Delhi | Singapore | Washington DC | Melbourne

Advance Praise

If you can dream it, you can do it. This book helps you dream and gives you a toolkit on how to turn those dreams to reality by reprogramming and refreshing your thinking. It helps you in believing in yourselves and making your dreams come alive. This book literally opens up a toolkit of possibilities; all you have to do is to visualize and believe you can do it. I am a product of believing in possibilities and making them happen. This is a must-read book for entrepreneurs, leaders, managers, and anyone who wishes to achieve anything.

Anurag Batra
Entrepreneur, Media Mogul, TV Show Host,
Author, and Angel Investor

The book *The Law of Possibilities* is one of the best inspirational books I have come across in the recent past. It suggests how one can create one's own future by letting worries and fears vanish and fade away. It is possible to realize dreams and to experience joy and happiness. It reinforces the fact "what you give FOCUS, ENERGY, and ATTENTION to becomes a reality" and that "THOUGHT, FAITH, and PRACTICE can change things for the better." A must read for anyone who wants to make things happen.

H. R. Mohan
Past President, Computer Society of India and
IEEE Computer Society

The Law of Possibilities will help you transform your life and get results that you thought were simply not possible before. Anne-Mette's words will help bring a sea change in your life to help you climb the highest mountains and swim across the deepest oceans with ease.

Saptarshi Roy
Business Lead (India), InterActive; Former Director, Laureate Higher Education Group and Universitas 21 Global

With The Law of Possibilities, you can achieve what you thought was not possible before. The book will inspire you to become an energized performer and also become a better human being.

Raja Dasgupta
Founder and CEO, Studenting Era

The Law of Possibilities is a new law of life that will take you beyond mere survival in this world. It will take you to the zone of performance and help you transform into a new human being.

Shefali Walia
CEO, Wetravelsolo

This is a landmark book that will help you make your life beautiful. It will inspire you for greatness.

Siddharth Jain

CEO, Discovery Education

The Law of Possibilities is an interesting book that encourages positive thinking by emphasizing the impact of the power of our thoughts on the outcome of our lives. It has the potential to instill confidence and faith in the readers to steer their life towards achieving their aspirations.

Promil Pande
Former Dean, School of Fashion and Design, GD Goenka University

THE LAW OF
POSSIBILITIES

IT IS THE POWER WITHIN
YOU THAT MAKES THINGS
HAPPEN—THE CHOICE IS YOURS!

THE LAW OF POSSIBILITIES
HOW TO GET WHAT YOU WANT

ANNE-METTE RØSTING

Los Angeles | London | New Delhi
Singapore | Washington DC | Melbourne

Copyright © Anne-Mette Røsting, 2018

All rights reserved. No part of this book may be reproduced or utilized in any form or by any means, electronic or mechanical, including photocopying, recording or by any information storage or retrieval system, without permission in writing from the publisher.

First published in 2018 by

SAGE Publications India Pvt Ltd
B1/I-1 Mohan Cooperative Industrial Area
Mathura Road, New Delhi 110 044, India
www.sagepub.in

SAGE Publications Inc
2455 Teller Road
Thousand Oaks, California 91320, USA

SAGE Publications Ltd
1 Oliver's Yard, 55 City Road
London EC1Y 1SP, United Kingdom

SAGE Publications Asia-Pacific Pte Ltd
3 Church Street
#10-04 Samsung Hub
Singapore 049483

Published by Vivek Mehra for SAGE Publications India Pvt Ltd, typeset in 13/15 Garamond by Fidus Design Pvt. Ltd., Chandigarh and printed at Chaman Enterprises, New Delhi.

Library of Congress Cataloging-in-Publication Data
Name: Rosting, Anne-Mette, 1955- author.
Title: The law of possibilities : how to get what you want / Anne-Mette Rosting.
Description: Thousand Oaks : SAGE Publications Inc, [2018] | Includes bibliographical references.
Identifiers: LCCN 2017049051| ISBN 9789352805723 (pbk : alk. paper) | ISBN 9789352805730 (epub 2.0)
Subjects: LCSH: Possibility—Psychological aspects. | Success. | Positive psychology.
Classification: LCC BF723.P67 R67 2018 | DDC 158—dc23 LC record available at https://lccn.loc.gov/2017049051

ISBN: 978-93-528-0572-3 (PB)

SAGE Team: Manisha Mathews, Priya Arora, Madhurima Thapa and Ritu Chopra

Dedicated to my fantastic husband, Jørn, and my wonderful sons, Marius and Christoffer, with whom I enjoy sharing my life and who graciously let me have the summer vacation for this exciting project

Thank you for choosing a SAGE product!
If you have any comment, observation or feedback,
I would like to personally hear from you.

Please write to me at **contactceo@sagepub.in**

Vivek Mehra, Managing Director and CEO, SAGE India.

Bulk Sales

SAGE India offers special discounts
for purchase of books in bulk.
We also make available special imprints
and excerpts from our books on demand.

For orders and enquiries, write to us at

Marketing Department
SAGE Publications India Pvt Ltd
B1/I-1, Mohan Cooperative Industrial Area
Mathura Road, Post Bag 7
New Delhi 110044, India

E-mail us at **marketing@sagepub.in**

Get to know more about SAGE

Be invited to SAGE events, get on our mailing list.
Write today to **marketing@sagepub.in**

This book is also available as an e-book.

CONTENTS

Foreword by Liv Arnesen	ix
Preface	xi
Acknowledgments	xxi
The Law of Possibilities	1
The Possibility-virus and the Possibility-agent	18
How The Law of Possibilities Works	27
Humility and Gratitude	63
Possibility-rules	72
Possibility-possibilities	82
Ten Inspiring Possibilities	99
Taking Action	149
Five Possibilities for the More Experienced	157
Why Is This Book for You?	184
A Bit about Everything	192
Sources of Inspiration	194
About the Author	195

FOREWORD

I have been deeply and profoundly touched by the contents of this book and even more so by being asked to write the foreword for it.

For more than nine years in her country, Norway, Anne-Mette has touched people's lives with this book about The Law of Possibilities, and she still does. With this book, she has inspired a lot of people around Norway to better their leadership and life. She has also prevented people from suicide, lowered people's blood pressure, and helped medicated people to take responsibilities for their lives and become happy family members without the help of medication.

Anne-Mette has described it all in this soul-searching book, and additionally, she gives you tools for taking actions. I encourage you to read it carefully and thoughtfully with a mind that is open to having many of your beliefs challenged through a new way of thinking and acting according to the personal experiences from people she has inspired, coached, or touched by her presence.

Anne-Mette is changing the people she meets in her personal space as well as in the corporate world and makes them open up to new ways of living by providing them with intuitive visionary insights into her approach to life.

This book has an exceptional energy that helps you see possibilities in your own life. It focuses on a transforming theme in a simple and trustworthy way.

This book is filled with so much love that will give you a renewed sense of who you truly are, why you are the changemaker in your own and other people's lives, and how you can transcend any fear that holds you back and defines your everyday life. Anne-Mette's life experiences are very much reflected in the fact that you are about to read her book. She shows you how important thoughts are that create your words and lead your actions.

The Law of Possibilities is a simple but powerful book about living that inspires all readers. May you take Anne-Mette's words to your heart and live them joyfully in your everyday life in this world.

Enjoy this wonderful book with a great message to all humans!

Liv Arnesen
Polar Explorer, Educator, and Lecturer

Preface

Always look at the bright side of life ...
—Eric Idle

Put simply, you can say that there are two roads to choose in life—you can choose the road of light, filled with happiness and possibilities, or you can choose the road of darkness where negativity and problems are in focus. Of course, there will be nuances and combinations of these extremes, but this book is all about life in the light. This book is meant to inspire you to see all the opportunities you have if you choose the light. To inspire you to find a feeling of happiness, while making yourself aware that you possess lots of resources, that you are creative and a sound human being, fully capable of making your own choices.

You should also know that within you are all the facets of light and darkness, but the most important part of all is which side of you, you choose to express, at any given time. Who do you want to be? How do you want to live your life? Make up your mind and practice wishing for what you want out of life. Don't bother with everyone else, but look at yourself. Who are you now and what do you know you have the potential of becoming? Make your choices, focus, increase your consciousness, and begin traveling along your road. It's right there in front of you, right now—find your true identity. Do not bother looking back at what has happened before in your life. Just look ahead and make sure you are always moving toward your natural powerful potential. If you think it's hard or you're unsure of how to get started, ask someone for help. There are lots of good helpers out there. You, my fellow human being, have been put here on earth to enjoy life, to be happy, to grow and learn, not to struggle. You are way too valuable to do that.

For many years, I've had lots of experiences that I found to be incredibly exciting. My inherent curiosity had brought me many experiences that I used to think just happened by chance, but now I know the name of it. It is the law of attraction. I find it to be much more energizing to use the name "The Law of Possibilities." I've always been a seeking and curious person, one who would never take no for an answer, one who has always had a life philosophy that everything is possible. I have preferred to have my own experiences through doing things, rather than just listening to others and rejecting something without even trying it. The choices that I have made have not always been valuable to me, but I still have always chosen to approach challenges and hardships with the perspective of "What will I learn from this?" For me, it has simply been much more important to search for the positive, to think positive thoughts, to try to stay positive, and to see all the possibilities that lie ahead. Even when faced with challenges in life, I have tried to view them as possibilities in disguise. It has not always been easy, because after all, I too am only human. Life might be a bumpy ride, but one of the most important things I have learned is that when I was at my lowest, I learned the most; it was there that my personal growth and development mostly took place.

The Law of Possibilities came to me during a time in my life when my children were young and I was facing lots of challenges. Coincidentally, an e-mail appeared in my inbox from a very dear friend of mine, who at around the same time had just finished her training to be a personal coach. Someone she knew in her coaching network needed clients for practice. She needed to be able to document a certain number of hours with customers to pass her exam. Saying yes just came naturally to me. I would be more than happy to help that person pass her exam, not to mention the opportunity to help myself develop even further. The challenges I was facing made it especially easy to say yes. Here, I would be able to get help from someone and it would be wonderful to talk to someone beside my family, someone who could give me another perspective and who would understand me.

During my coaching, I was introduced to The Law of Possibilities. My coach did so with great enthusiasm. It didn't really interest me as much then as it does now. I remember her telling me about the law. She continuously asked me "What is it that you want?" What did I want? Could I have everything I ever wished for, when my entire world just seemed like this gigantic challenge? Later, I understood that the law was just as new to the coach at that time, as it was to me, and that she herself was in a learning process regarding the use of the law—she didn't "own" it yet.

Because of that, she could not get the true meaning of the message through to me. It's also possible that I wasn't ready for it then. That's just how it was. But now I know better, because the words of the law did something to me anyway. Through the words of the law, I discovered I had been introduced to a reality that I had practiced my entire life, without even knowing it. This new awareness gave me a huge "aha" experience, which later on led me to a more active use of the law, in a new and much more concrete fashion. I now have one of many tools that I can use for the rest of my life. I am completely certain, beyond a shadow of doubt, about what I want to bring with me, as I go on in life. I have the same wishes for you as the reader of this book.

Early on, in my first job after my studies, I learned just how valuable it is to be able to accept challenges, even if they seemed more demanding than I ever thought I would be able to handle. The fantastic feeling of achievement I experienced when I mastered those challenges was quite amazing. I quickly discovered I could handle a whole lot more than I first thought, if I just made the decision and made up my mind to do it. It has always been easier for me to agree to something than to recognize my limitations along the way. I must admit that it is not always such a good idea to agree to something without first checking your feelings about it.

In addition, I gradually learned that it does matter a lot what kind of energy I put into things. I can do everything I put my mind to and simultaneously I get a feel for whether my intuition is right for me or not.

My first boss was a great man in many ways. He would throw me in at the deep end and then tell me to swim! He even did it without first teaching me the "strokes." I have no idea if this method is still in use today, but I have only one word to describe it: brutal. In retrospect, I will thankfully add that it was incredibly instructive and educational. I can remember telling myself that it is ok to start swimming, even if you can't see the shore on the other side of the ocean. I have always been sure of one thing—I will never drown as long as I keep on going. I have always had the ability and the willpower to stay afloat. It has all been about focus and endurance.

This type of learning demands that the spirit push through and that one be curious, both of which I was good at. With that said, this boss also happened to be one of the best I had during my entire career; he was the right one for me. What I got was full freedom with full responsibility. It gave me an incredible amount of growth, personal development, and experience that have stayed with me ever since, throughout the rest of my life.

During this period of my life, I got in touch with experiences that I myself created. It started once on my way to an important meeting. I was well prepared for it, but for some reason or another—and I honestly can't remember—while staring into my own eyes in the rearview mirror of my car, I told myself: "You can do this, you will do magnificent work and this meeting will bring you a new customer." I got the customer, and I came to think of what I had told myself back in the car. Coincidences? Back then, that's what I would have said. With the discovery I made, feeling so excited, I decided to try it again. And it worked, again. And again. A new way of thinking was born within me. I could influence the outcome of the situation I was about to enter by deciding in advance. Clever, right? This was yet another discovery of the phenomenon I want to share with you in my book, so that you too can have the chance of having similar experiences in your life.

This was just the start of a period of experimentation. That's what I must call it, even though I now know better. I had just started using The Law of Possibilities. By using this law, incredible opportunities will open to you, enabling you to achieve your dreams, big or small. It is a law that is clearly defined and easy to follow once your focus and awareness are in order. My way of increasing my awareness was to find new areas in which to test my discovery.

I could be doing presentations or lectures, something that I enjoy doing. The once shy and humble little girl I was as a child was now on center stage and loving it. This is when I really felt alive. But let's go back to when I first started doing lectures. I knew that if I wore my red jacket, I would get in touch with a power that convinced me that once I got on the stage, everything would be ok. I felt safe, my uneasiness was gone, and everything would go as it should. I also discovered that colors do things for me. Nowadays I don't need the red jacket anymore. Now I can wear whatever I want. I can go on stage and I am right on track, at once. It doesn't matter whether I am speaking to an audience of 20 or 300. I flourish; it gives me energy and makes me feel good. I am also sure that the basis for thriving on stage was founded way back when that red jacket meant a lot to me. Today I understand how my thoughts connect with those good feelings.

Something else that worked for me was music. I would be in my car, headed for a meeting, the music of Tina Turner blaring from the stereo. It's only Tina that could give that kind of an energy kick, and besides, I could sing along as loud as I wanted to without anyone hearing me. I must have arrived at my meetings more or less electric. No matter what, it gave me the power I needed to get my message across. Today, I do it completely different; now it's all about quietness, visualization, and making myself feel good. The techniques that I have shared with you up until now, such as visualization, colors, and music—could there even be more?

I also discovered that I could decide in advance where I would find an available parking space even in the middle of downtown, and it worked every time. Believe it or not, but there was always an available space for me, usually right in front of the door of where I was going, in the middle of downtown.

These kinds of situations happen when I have decided the outcome in advance and sent out a wish for what I would like to achieve. It has worked ever since. As you understand, this has become a way of life for me, a way of life that I find both magical and incredibly valuable. Other ingredients such as trust, love, thankfulness, and humility do have to be added to the formula to make the law work in its best way, something that I will come back to.

I enjoy working on my own personal development just as much as I like helping both you and others. It became clearer to me when I found the book *Ask and It is Given* written by Esther and Jerry Hicks; they describe how "equal attracts equal." This is a message that I in my own way wish to bring out into this world—to you and to others—in a simple and honest style that helps you understand how this is also attainable for you in a way that inspires you to start experimenting, so that you too can find out how to use The Law of Possibilities to make a difference in your life.

Without even knowing it, I had been speaking about this law during my lectures, because a few years ago I found a quote that made a strong impression on me. Henry Ford has said, "Whether you think you can do it, or you can't do it, you're right." This is The Law of Possibilities just phrased in other words. Throughout history, lots of great personalities have used this law without it ever being described or interpreted. In retrospect, I have found that great personalities such as Einstein, Newton, Beethoven, Edison, Lincoln, Shakespeare, and several other historically important people have been practicing the law in one form or another.

The movie and the book *The Secret* about the law of attraction has also found its way into my life and confirmed to me that the discoveries I made years ago were but experiences with The Law of Possibilities. Now that it has a name, it has become easier to relate to it as a deliberate way of living.

The Law of Possibilities is a law that I make use of every day, and it has become a very precious part of my life. This is a law that is so great and prized that I also want you to discover its magical powers, so that it can make your days even better and help you in finding the life you truly wish and dream of. Through practicing this law, you will learn how you can look forward to each and every day and to enjoy it to its fullest, rather than fighting against it. That's when you can live a life according to, and in harmony with, your innermost values, without being sidetracked by distracting influences.

If you do so, you'll be a lot more satisfied with yourself. And when you are more satisfied with yourself and find life enjoyable, you will be able to positively affect others around you, who in turn will positively affect others around themselves. This is how this law will reach out to the entire world. Together we will make the world a better place. There certainly has to be lots of other people out there, apart from me, with the vision of doing something good for the human race and something great for our society. We can do so by actively and consciously applying The Law of Possibilities.

Together we can work to make peace with ourselves and bring peace in the world. There's nothing you can't be, do, or get while you are a part of humanity. It's all about how you relate to yourself, how you relate to others, how others relate to you and other fellow human beings in society.

With this, I hope you will find this book to be so inspiring that it also brings you into action. Can the contents of this book really be true? The only way of finding out how The Law of Possibilities works is through your own experiences with it—so stop reading and thinking about it, and simply start to act in accordance with the law and make it a part of your life.

Make The Law of Possibilities your way of life.

ACKNOWLEDGMENTS

As I was approaching the end of this book about The Law of Possibilities, I discovered that I had realized one of my most important life journeys.

You have made me sort through, dive deeply into, and grow into all of the wisdom I have learned so far along my path of life. For me, you are the one who challenged me four years ago, when I thought that writing was "a piece of cake," but then no words were able to come out from my mind and onto my sheets of paper. Again, you were there two years later, wondering if I had thought some more about writing. At that time, you hit another string of mine, which led me to attend writing workshops so that I would be prepared to start my "writing journey." At the same time, those writing workshops taught me to be humble, humble about the fact that writing is an artistic expression which involves a lot of work. My redemption came one day in January four years after you challenged me the first time. That was the first time I knew what my heart was so full of. So full that it was almost spilling over in desire to share this with others, to make their every day easier.

You didn't give up in your attempts to get me to get closer to my own truth. Now I understand why you did it, and I am deeply grateful and thankful to you. You have given me the possibility to sort through my own insights and make them even more visible to me. Today, these insights are some of my most valuable possessions of my life, and they will stay with me forever. These insights have made me decide to live the rest of my life in the light, and at the same time, I want to share my insights with people who are willing to receive them.

Because of these insights—that I so joyfully share with others—this book is dedicated to you, Øystein, my guidance counselor.

Also a special thanks to,
My beautiful editors at Gyldendal, Jorunn and Anne Britt, who discovered me and my thoughts; to Rune who translated the Norwegian version to English for his American wife to read; Liam who quality assured the language in the English version. Thank you to the explorer Liv who has written the Foreword; a special thanks to June and Vibeke who made me shine for the new photos to be taken and at last but not least, Kapil who found me and opened the door to SAGE Publishing in New Delhi. A warm heartfelt thanks to you all.

Lastly, I thank

> All the people I have been so lucky to coach.
> All the people who have attended the classes I have held.
> All the companies that have hired me to hold inspiring lectures.
> Meeting and conference organizers that have engaged me to hold lectures and workshops.
> The adepts that I have mentored.
> All the exciting people I have met.
> All of you have in one way or another contributed to making this book possible.
> And of course thank you to the Norwegian public who made the book a bestseller and made *The Law of Possibilities* ready for its travel into the world.

Thank you very, very much!

For me, in my life, everything is possible, obstacles often are possibilities in disguise, and life itself is the greatest possibility of all. You may contact me at: post@naturalforce.no

The Law of Possibilities

The things you focus on and give your energy and attention to will become a reality, whether you want them or not.

So what do you want, really?

> **THE LAW HAS VERY FEW WORDS AND CONSISTS OF JUST THREE STEPS:**
> 1. Define your dream
> 2. Increase the frequencies—believe it's possible
> 3. Allow it to happen

You Already Have Experiences with The Law of Possibilities

You must surely have already experienced that something you needed in your life came to you at precisely the right moment. Or that you got a phone call from someone exactly the day you thought you would, even from someone you haven't been in touch with lately. Or that you bump into a person you've been thinking of recently. You certainly must have felt the feeling of being in the right place at the right time. All of these experiences are proof that The Law of Possibilities already exists in your life.

Maybe you've even heard of people in bad relationships, one partner after another, yet they always complain that they seem to attract the wrong kind of partner every time.

The Law of Possibilities works for them too because it delivers both what they wish for and what they don't wish for.

With this book, you will gain a deeper understanding of why things that happen, happen the way they do. After reading it, you will also be able to attract more of the things you want to do, know, or dream of, so that you can have more of the things you want and less of the things you don't want. It's that easy, but coincidentally, so hard. Everything is up to you, your focus, your awareness, and your choices.

Every time you make a choice, you change the future.

What is the Origin of The Law of Possibilities?

Energies are everywhere, all of the time, and can never be destroyed. You are energy, the people around you are energy, the phone you use is energy. The bicycle you ride on, the pet you love, the bread you eat, the money you earn, the work you do—everything you do is and has energy. Now you might understand why the outcomes of what you will achieve in life is all about what kind of energies you initially add to it, and that's what this book is all about—the energies with which you nourish your mind and your thoughts.

The energies are always available to make The Law of Possibilities effective. Energies are, in other words, the basic physiological explanation of positive and negative thinking, which is also the thing that is going to make The Law of Possibilities work for you.

A Little Bit about Energies

A little bit of facts might clarify the basics of what we describe as energy, or positive and negative thinking, if that's what you want to call it, which in turn will affect your experience with The Law of Possibilities. I am by no means a physicist, so I will have to rely on the knowledge of the great masters and their explanations.

There is a maxim in physics that "energy cannot be created or destroyed." Energy just exists and can only be transformed from one form into another. You may want to know this to help you understand why The Law of Possibilities works: it is based on the fact that the energy you emit will return to you.

Source: Concept by author, drawn by Torunn Berge.

I myself am humbled by what energy is and what it does and will try to explain it to you as simply as I can. I can feel and sense energies throughout all aspects of life.

According to Albert Einstein, energy transference between two bodies occurs through quantum physics, by a number of quanta. Particle I delivers energy to particle II, and their energy frequency is the number of oscillations per second between the two of them. He also saw light as carrying specific amount of energy and named the energy particles photons.

Louis de Broglie was the first one to claim that a mass too can display wavelike characteristics, which later was proved by Clinton Davies in 1925. That is why both particles and light are considered quantum objects, and that the speed of light is the highest velocity attainable. Both waves and particles are equal descriptions of quantum objects. To understand this, we have to make use of two models. That does not imply that they are two different things, but just that there are two different approaches to explaining something that we cannot see through our "biological glasses." Compare it with the fact that water is still water, whether it takes the shape of ice, water, or steam. It is all water, although it displays different characteristics and properties.

Einstein said that "mathematical theory is certain, but practical math is uncertain." The journey goes further, to France in 1982, to what is known as the aspect experiment where the researchers were able to prove that two quantum particles that once were attached and then separated by vast distances would still be connected to each other in one way or another. If one particle changed, so did the other, and they even did it simultaneously.

Scientists are still yet uncertain of how the mechanics involved in these changes occur, but what is really exciting is how the explanations of the laws of nature also applies in our context, which shows how each atom of the human body constantly responds to influences, whether we can sense it or not. (As a curious human being, I wonder if this could be the explanation to why a friend of mine might get in touch with me the same day I think of her, because I no longer think this happens by coincidence anymore.)

Because of this, it can be a very profound perspective to assume and believe that there is something more between the heavens and the earth than what just meets our eyes and that we might be able to explain logically at all times. Even if the aspect experiment is closing in on explaining it to all of you that need scientific proof to accept The Law of Possibilities, you too can even make meaningful steps for yourself. Try to become "a little scientist" of your own, with regard to your own life, by applying the law, testing it, and making your own experiences. By applying attraction in this manner, you will be able to collect important energies within you and around you so that you too can make incredible accomplishments and make the impossible possible.

It is the power of your thoughts that make things happen.

The Law of Possibilities is not a new law. What is new is that the law has received renewed attention in ways that makes it more credible and attainable for both you and me. It is said that this way of thinking originates way back in history, to as long as back to 3000 BC, and that the Babylonians supposedly had inscriptions of this law engraved on blocks of stone.

The Law of Possibilities will affect the entire experience of your life. It will affect who you are and how you perceive things by how you choose your thoughts. It is you that will make the law work, through which thoughts you choose to think. My recommendation to you: as opposed to viewing energies from an intellectual point of view, go out and feel them, try to sense what energies are and what they can do to you. Now that you know that everything is energy, you can create your own experiences.

What you now will read about is the vast possibilities through positive thinking—those that will get you in touch with good and positive feelings that in turn will launch good and positive experiences in your life. A very exciting consideration is that you can actually learn to become optimistic—you can actually teach yourself optimistic behavior. One way of starting out is by finding out and becoming aware of how much energy you really do put into being pessimistic. After all, you do live in a world filled with opportunities, right?

> *In its most fantastic form, The Law of Possibilities is also a way of life and a beautiful form of performing art.*

In this book, you will find different stories of possibilities, told in a light and cheerful mixture of experiences, thoughts, and curiosity. The possibilities are presented in a way that you can make direct use of them, or perhaps they can give you ideas about how you can try out your own possibilities. The possibilities of this book may be utilized as a foundation for you to build your own important house of possibilities, an inspiration to explore your own curiosity in a childish, playful manner. Let the possibilities in this book give you the inspiration and the knowledge you need to make these possibilities into a lifestyle, a way of living your life that always brings you to where you dream to be, as a possibility-agent actively practicing The Law of Possibilities.

Energy Frequencies

The Law of Possibilities is unique in its own form, and you will not need any other tools besides yourself, clarity, and a good portion of faith laced with a few sprinkles of happiness. Send your skepticism and your doubts off on vacation during the time you decide to incorporate The Law of Possibilities into your life and become a happy, playful, enterprising possibility-agent. Maybe you'll never ever face the skepticism and the doubts again. But who cares? I've heard some people talk about something they call healthy skepticism too, but what in the world is healthy about skepticism? For me, that is just a negative frequency that only attracts more skepticism.

To make you understand the law better, I am going to introduce the term "frequency" or "radiance," if you wish. I will be using both of these terms, switching between them. Frequencies are the vibrations that you can sense, feel within your body, and that your surroundings can sense too. Sometimes we are not aware of the fact that our surroundings can sense how we are doing. But other people are perceiving creatures too, some more than others, and we are all just basically quantum particles in contact. No matter what, there only exist two kinds of radiance or feelings: either the frequencies are negative or positive. It is all up to you and the mode you choose your senses to be in. Pay attention that I say "choose to be in," because you have a choice.

FREQUENCIES	
POSITIVE	NEGATIVE
Happiness	Disappointment
Love	Loneliness
Enthusiasm	Lack of enthusiasm
Cheerfulness	Sadness
Pride	Confusion
Wellness	Stress
Well-being	Wounded

As I am sure you understand it is important to be aware of what you radiate, because no matter what you radiate, The Law of Possibilities will give you more of the same. So what is it you want more of?

What is it that starts the frequencies? They start with a thought. The frequencies start with the thought that you have chosen to think. When you have chosen a thought and spice it with the feeling behind that thought, the radiance starts. That is why it is so important to choose the appropriate thoughts, thoughts that nourish your desired result, and naturally it makes a difference whether you choose to think a positive or a negative thought. The Law of Possibilities will just give you more of the negative if that's what you choose or more of the positive if you find that to be of more importance. When you have chosen a thought and are adding the corresponding feelings to it, you are capable of deciding which feelings you want to fit in with that thought. If you repeat and practice the combination of thoughts and feelings, it will be stored in your consciousness, and eventually, it becomes your own association. Some associations you carry with you might have been created as early as in your childhood or from situations when you have had appropriate or inappropriate experiences. But everything is possible to change, absolutely everything is possible; you just have to make the decision to teach yourself new and more appropriate associations in situations where you have gone astray. Again, what do you want more of?

To better understand that everything is energy and that energies move in circles, it could be worthwhile to know that thoughts are energies as well. In addition to your thoughts, everything you feel, say, or do are forms of energy. Therefore, both you and I are in an exchange of energies every moment of our lives.

Thoughts envision goals and dreams, feelings shape reactions, words become decisions, and actions create your experiences. That's exactly why your thoughts, your feelings, what you say and do in every moment, and the things that you radiate, even the responses that come back to you, will be creating your sense of reality. Each and every one of us creates our own destiny, even though you at times would like to give that responsibility to someone else. Take a moment to reflect on what you yourself have put in motion to experience the things you are experiencing at this very instant.

Why Don't We Ask For the Things We Dream of Right Away?

There could be so many reasons why you don't already have all the things you are dreaming of or wishing for. One thing is certain: it is not because of coincidences or that you have been unlucky. Maybe these are thoughts that you already have had, with which you have given your energy. Let us have a closer look at things that might have stood in the way for you to be able to achieve your dreams. There are five barriers that might show up when we ask for something, and the first one is:

Lack of Knowledge

Maybe you don't even know what to ask for because you don't know what is available for you or maybe you are not enough in touch with yourself and your potentials that you are not capable of noticing your true needs and wishes. Or maybe you don't even know how to ask, because so far you have not had any good role models at home, at school, or at your workplace. Maybe you are one of those that don't know who or how to ask? You have not learned how you can ask for a hug, a piece of advice, or how to make a breakthrough for what you have to offer. Your body language tells, even without words, whether "I'm with you" or "not right now."

A lot of your lack of knowledge can go back as far as to your childhood, when you may have been ignored, rejected, or felt shame regarding communicating your own wishes. You may have tried to express your wishes and dreams but discovered that it felt safer not to. Maybe you have even buried your wishes from fear of your parents, other grown-ups, or reactions to them. The end result could have turned out to be that you've stopped looking for what you really wish for and feel that it is easier to respond with an: "I don't know" or "It doesn't matter." Most people have rarely or never had good role models when it comes to asking direct questions, or to ask for what they felt they needed, or even what they wished for more than anything in this world.

A System of Belief That Is Limiting or Unclear

The second barrier between asking for some of the things you want could be due to the fact that a limiting or negative faith in yourself has crept into your subconsciousness, controlling your actions and possibly preventing you from believing that you can actually achieve your dreams.

> *Everything we are is a result of our thoughts.*
> —Dhammapada

Now that you are told that you are born as a free spirit void of any kind of preprogramming, where does that programming come from? The answer might be a bit given, it comes from outside influences—from your parents, your teachers, your peers, or for that matter, even from the media, and from the fact that you allow it to happen. We are also taught that is better to give than to receive, and simultaneously, you may be afraid of disappointment. In this way, you have learned that your desires aren't all that important.

Try to think through how it is that you can get what you want if you don't even know what it is you wish for. You have to change your programming. The Law of Possibilities is there to help you make your dreams come true, but possibly you first need to practice identifying your dreams. It's as easy as if you wish for more love, attention, friends, help, or whatever it is that you want, you have to start by presenting your wish and dare to ask for it. How about adding a little bit of prompting techniques into your daily routine as a way of approaching your dreams?

There is a saying that goes: "Be careful what you wish for, because you just might get it." That statement has a negative charge, but by using of The Law of Possibilities, you can easily turn it into the opposite. The Law of Possibilities says: "Equal attracts equal" or "You always get what you ask for." The sayings say the same, but the latter way of expressing it gives you the option of choosing whether you want to go with the negative approach, or the positive, just like the law does. You'll get the positivity if you choose positive frequencies. How do you want to think?

Fear

The third barrier could be fear—the fear of failure, the fear of not being liked by other people, the fear of choosing what you really want.

It is only your mind that can create fear. The result of fear is usually being passive.

You might be satisfied with less than what you really dream of, and you might, as well, end up judging those who achieve the same goals as you are dreaming of. You might lack the courage you need to ask or even lack the things you need to create and succeed. You end up spending all your energy protecting yourself from the fears you have crafted, instead of using your energy to create your dreams.

> **THERE MIGHT BE LOTS OF THINGS YOU FEAR, SO THINK IT THROUGH AND SEE IF YOU CAN RECOGNIZE AND IDENTIFY YOURSELF WITH SOME OF THESE FEARS:**
>
> The fear of acting stupid
>
> The fear of not having enough energy
>
> The fear of being punished
>
> The fear of endless discussions

You can get rid of anything that impedes you in life, no matter what it is, but you may have to practice thinking new and appropriate thoughts to get past the inappropriate ones.

Low Self-esteem

This is the fourth barrier that might prevent you from achieving your dreams. Are you one of those people that don't think it is possible to create the life you want? All the great personalities of our society or the people that have made it or achieved something that has been noticed by others, they have all made it there because they believed in their faith and their courage, and they were hardly held back from any of the barriers mentioned above. Could it be that you are one of those that believe that the needs of others are more important than your own—especially the needs of your children, the needs of your elderly parents, the needs of your boss, the needs of the homeless, or the needs of those who really need it? Are you among those who sacrifice their own needs on someone else's altar? Are you someone's doormat, instead of standing up for yourself and listening to your own feelings?

If your feelings are not acknowledged by those who are the most important people in your life, it could be that you conclude that your own wishes and dreams aren't important enough. Low self-esteem is best compared with putting all your energies into your outer superficial world, to people, things, and experiences that are beyond you, at the expense of your own real requirements.

The last barrier that you might have been in touch with, and that might have prevented you from getting familiar with The Law of Possibilities, is:

Pride

Some people are so proud that they become stuck in their own pride and turn too arrogant to acknowledge their own needs for something or someone. To stop to ask for advice or help from others really becomes completely unthinkable. Your sole conviction is that you have to do everything yourself to make it right, or rather perfect. Preferably, you even have to make it in your very first attempt too, if not you risk losing respect, friendships, or your own conviction of what has to be the right "standards." You are always right and so sure of yourself that when you, for instance, have acquired a new electronic gadget of some kind, you start installing it without even checking the instructions. Checking the instructions are for sissies, it only being worth the paper it is printed on when you finally reach the point of total frustration and simply cannot figure out how to do it. In reality, you are just a member of the gang of independent individuals that rather suffer in silence than asking for help.

To ask for help will truly change your life. Making mistakes brings gifts too—the worst thing that could possibly happen is that you learn from your mistakes, develop yourself, and grow.

Now you know that the three most important obstructions blocking the road, preventing you from living a harmonious and good life, are:

1. Impatience—because you will always have enough time. If you change your mind and realize that time comes, it doesn't go, you will always have enough of it. Don't cut it into pieces, forging ahead in your life with thoughts filled with everything to have to get done, and that nothing moves fast enough.

2. Perfectionism—because what you are or do will be good enough. It is sufficient and adequate by far. And what is perfect really? It is nothing but how you, in your mind, have defined as the only way. There are always possibilities for you to achieve your wishes on so many different levels. You won't believe how your thoughts are fantastic tools to do just that.

3. Being a workaholic—probably the only form of substance abuse that is socially accepted.

   The more you work the better employee you are. But do you work a lot because of the pure and sheer joy it brings you, or do you do it because you, or others, expect it of you? Do you feel a rush from everything you accomplish, or have you even forgotten that feeling? Sometimes your body will let you know, trying to help you, by saying: Stop it! I can't do it anymore, because your thoughts and how you feel doesn't quite match up. You might experience being burned out.

JUST LIKE IMPATIENCE, PERFECTIONISM, AND BEING A WORKAHOLIC CAN BLOCK YOUR PATH OF LIVING A BETTER LIFE, THERE ARE ALSO THREE EXCELLENT ATTITUDES THAT WILL BRING HAPPINESS TO YOUR LIFE:

- By thinking wholesome and good thoughts
- By speaking in wholesome and good words
- By letting all your actions and deeds become wholesome and good

This again will lead you to a wonderful life, if you allow yourself to be open to learning processes and always encourage others to do the same.

Allow yourself to be open to earn a living in the world and always encourage others to do the same.

Don't fret and grieve over longing for the true beauty of life and also help others to find the beauty within themselves.

What Makes The Law of Possibilities Important?

The Law of Possibilities has shown that:

- You can discover the fantastic potential within yourself.
- You can really get to know yourself.
- What you believe is impossible, becomes possible.
- Tensions can loosen up.
- You can help yourself to become a star in the heavens of life.
- You will take better care of your health.
- Your dreams can become real.
- You will verify yourself as a valuable person.
- The law is easy to bring with you everywhere.
- It nourishes happiness and brings you more of it.
- It works everywhere and at any time of the day.
- You can attract the loved one you always have dreamed of.
- You can experience negativity turning into positivity.
- You can have the career of your dreams.
- You can discover that you actually can reach further than you thought.
- You can experience surprising yourself.
- You can discover that you affect the world around you in a positive way.
- Everyone can be a possibility-agent.
- The Law of Possibilities can be used by everyone, everywhere, at all times.

Anyone can become a possibility-agent. The only items you need are simply "thought," "faith," and "practice," and believe it or not, they are even free. It is your own efforts that create the results. And the more you practice a positive approach to The Law of Possibilities, the more you develop your own abilities, the more enthusiasm you will discover, and the better you will become at contaminating the world with possibility-viruses.

The Possibility-virus and the Possibility-agent

The possibility-virus is not a virus you can catch, but a virus that you have to allow and accept. This word is my playful contribution to new words that will be part of participating in creating something positive for our society.

The word "possibility-virus" is put together by joining the words "possibility" and "virus."

Possibilities because: everything is possible, absolutely anything is possible—it's solely about your thoughts of yourself and what's happening to you in life. The source of your opportunities are based on how strongly you believe in yourself, and the strength of your faith in what you wish for or what you dream of—the belief that starts with a thought and that nourishes your manifestations.

Virus because: viruses are contagious, viruses can last forever, viruses can last for just a little while, viruses can be treated, and viruses do harm to your body.

The most important thing of all is that this virus, the possibility-virus, has the intention of infecting many people, and with a lifelong, lasting effect. It will feel good to have this virus in your body and the virus is completely dependent on you as a person so as to be able to thrive and develop. Without you filling yourself with bubbly, playful possibility-viruses, you will have very little to share with others. You already have this virus dormant within you and you have had it all of your life. The virus is your thoughts and your feelings that can make every day playful and bubbly. This virus can bring you happiness in all areas of your life, change your life completely, and make your life into a wonderful magical experience.

This is what Solvår experienced when she heard of the word for the very first time:

My Instant Reaction

- When I heard the word possibility-virus, I visually experienced it as sparklers in my head.
- I noticed that I began smiling—the word gave me energy.
- I immediately pictured how the possibility-virus can speedily start spreading itself throughout our entire population because there isn't any vaccination against this virus.
- In the latest Sunday paper, there was an article about young people wanting to establish their own businesses—they too can be infected by the possibility-virus.

Possibility-virus Regards from Solvar

The possibility-virus has to be the best virus to become infected with in this world. It has to be the only positive epidemic the world has ever seen or heard of, the only one that is worth receiving with pleasure, and that we would love to see on the cover story of every newspaper.

Similarly, a possibility-agent is a person that lives, exists, and contaminates others with the possibility-virus and in this way confirms their faith in the law. The possibility-agent is someone that has made up their mind and that person might just as well be you.

The Right Side of Your Brain, Your Good Samaritan

Your brain is, if you like, just like an intricate and sophisticated computer. It is useful for us to have a little peek inside it to get a better understanding of how to put the law into use. What is it that actually triggers the actions of a human being when he or she learns of new and important knowledge? What is it that makes us distinguish something as "exciting" and valuable to us and that makes us seek more knowledge and a deeper understanding of something that seems like unknown territory? As soon as we make the connection that something is interesting and exciting, what is it that actually fires up our "engine of change" that makes us want to explore this matter more? Or what is it that makes us realize that there is something about ourselves that we want to change? What is it that we humans need to make us start doing something, rather than just thinking about it?

The ability to utilize the right side of your brain is essential to start the process of living according to The Law of Possibilities. The more you are able to activate the right side of your brain, the better the possibilities will be for you to be able to visualize your dreams, to overcome the time thieves, and to facilitate a comprehensive picture of what it is you want to do and who you want to be in your life.

In the traditional school system of today, a logical way of thinking and a good approach to life is valued and honored. A child, as you once used to be, is initially naturally curious and in search of knowledge and wisdom. Just think back in time. Something happens to you as you walk through the school gates—unintentionally they take away your ability to play, your natural curiosity, in order to make you fit into the system. According to the UiO (University of Oslo, Department of Education, Faculty of Educational Sciences), all of their attention becomes directed toward facts and answers by the time the students reach the fourth or fifth grade. Their creativity becomes under stimulated. At this stage, the students have become a part of the system.

I can confirm this with my own experiences from doing lectures and classes. Amongst a group of about 50 grown-up people, I might possibly get two or three hands up in the air when I ask if there is anyone in the audience that, for example, knows how to draw a drawing or paint a picture. Much of this comes from their condemnation of their own abilities to be creative. This is clearly a state of mind that belongs in the outer superficial world, where it surely is more important what other people think of your creativity, rather than your own perception of it, or whether your performance is brilliant. Our thoughts are easily tainted by how we believe the outside world perceives us, which in turn easily turns into our system of belief. It is not about perfectionism, or whether something is ugly or something is pretty, it is all about your condemnation of yourself.

Think about this for a moment: if you will now make use of the law to direct all of your energy and attention toward becoming a great artist, there will be nothing in this world stopping you from doing it. A class might be what it takes to get you started and to develop your talents, but the most important thing is that you start increasing your awareness. The fact that you start creating and that others encourage you along the way will start positive thoughts within yourself. You will be headed along one of several possible paths of life. The possibilities are endless and it is all up to you to make use of your own creative abilities to go back to your own "home base," to get in touch with your inner potential.

The Two Sides of the Brain

The brain is divided into two sides, the right and the left. These two sides both have their own specialties.

The left side is the logical part. This side of the brain handles words and numbers; it is the part that enables us to figure out that two plus two equals four. It keeps track of things and amongst other things reminds us to pay our bills on time. It also enables us to form words into sentences. This part of the brain relates to specific topics, and it is the analyzing side of the brain.

The right side of the brain likes pictures and has much more freedom than the left side. It is the creative and intuitive part that can relate to several things at once. It is the multitasking part. The right side of the brain also has a very relaxed relationship concerning time, it just lets time come to it.

All people make use of both sides of their brains, but one side of the brain tends to be the most dominant one, and it is different from one person to another. The ideal situation would be if we were able to make use of both sides of our brain equally and just as much.

Then, when facing a certain situation, you would be able to first sense what the situation is and then find the most appropriate mechanism to deal with it. Most people choose to trust their most predominant brain half at all times and solve the situation with the tools they are used to and most comfortable with. This is also why different people might interpret the same situation through a different set of eyes, depending on which half of their brain is the most prevailing one. Abraham Maslow had a saying that goes: "He that is good with a hammer tends to think everything is a nail."

The most beautiful poem in life is the one that is lived while it is composed.

—Frederic Amiel

You should also know that our society has a preference for the left brain side where words, measuring, and logic is valued the most. It is also the side of the brain our school system favors where you have been taught and trained. That's why it is not surprising that there are more people mainly using the left part of their brain rather than those using their right half, who are creative, intuitive, and perceiving. These properties are often viewed as less important. But it doesn't always have to be like this forever and personally I believe that in the future there will be a need for people who will make more use of the right side of their brain. No matter what, the more aware you are of the different capacities of the different sides of the brain, the better you will be prepared to face your specific needs in a more effective manner.

In the same way, extraordinarily creative people can have an overly stimulated right side of their brain and thus are less in touch with the practical, logical left part of their brain. Everybody that does tend to have a more dominant brain side, whether it is the right one or the left one, would benefit from developing their opposite brain half to achieve a better balance in their life.

All great personalities and people that have achieved their dreams in life have had one thing in common. They have put their goals on paper and have then focused all of their effort and attention into accomplishing this goal. These people have found the drive to reach their dreams by following their own paths and by having faith in themselves and by paying attention to each and every signal, big or small, that has any kind of association to their dream. These people have hardly ever been motivated by a wish to make loads of money, but they have been so driven by the passion they have for what they are doing, that they have attracted what they have needed to achieve their goals. Just look at Oprah Winfrey, Bill Gates, J. K. Rowling, the band A-ha, Tiger Woods, Usain Bolt, Nargis Fakhri, and many more. Whether they have been familiar with The Law of Possibilities or not, I presume that they all have it in common and that they have been actively thinking positive thoughts. This is the same as using the law—that's how easy it is. I am sure their achievements have come as a result of them doing something that they have a genuine passion for. Something that was started as an idea was nourished repeatedly until it grew bigger, without them ever doubting that it could be made into reality. By using Usain Bolt as an example, I think you will agree with me that he didn't stand on the top of the victory podium the very first time he ever wore running shoes. He must surely have focused and focused again and practiced, without ever letting go of his dream. The dream of being on top of that victory podium, of being number one. Now that you are familiar with The Law of Possibilities, it is your turn to enjoy progress, improvement, and prosperity in your life. Whether you have big ideas, or smaller ones, make sure they are your own thoughts and not someone else's. Challenge your least dominant brain half, and create more balance for yourself.

How to Get Started?

It starts by recognizing that you are carrying the key to your own life yourself. You've got it right there in your pocket. The key is your own thoughts and feelings and you have had it in your hand all along. You've still got it and it will always be available.

Too many people in our part of the world are striving for success in the outer world. A lot of people want a successful career in their line of work, fine houses, and all sorts of material symbols of accomplishment. But these superficial symbols rarely bring us what research shows that we really want, which is happiness. We all want these outer superficial symbols, because we believe they will bring us happiness, but in reality it is exactly the opposite. First, we have to find inner happiness, an inner peace with ourselves, a vision or a dream, a goal. Then, all outer things will fall into place. Everything you want will simply become available as you work with your inner landscape; the world that surrounds us is just a world of effects created in your mind.

Another fantastic way of getting more in touch with yourself is by becoming more aware of how you spend your time and energy. We all have things that occupy our minds—health, our children, the environment, school, the news, aunts, uncles, friends, and studies. I could go on and on. I believe that you can quickly reason what occupies you right now, which are things that you aren't fully committed to. If you distinguish between these areas as arenas where you don't have any mental or emotional influence and choose to call these areas as "interesting, but unimportant," it will be easier for you to focus and point your energies in the right direction.

As you might understand by now, The Law of Possibilities gives you more of the things you feel or radiates: you will experience possibility-viruses as the positive version of the law and worry-viruses as the negative. So make sure that your frequencies for the most part are consisting of possibility-viruses so that you can find the happiness you might be looking for or hope to find in this book. Think through what it is that hits you or what it is that challenges you with this way of thinking. But do know:

This is not a law about receiving, but a law about allowing.

You have to allow yourself and dare to take your first step in a new direction, which at first might appear scary, strange, or different. No matter what, the first step is to figure out: what do I dream of? What is it that I dream of being, doing, or achieving in life?

How The Law of Possibilities Works

As a professional possibility-agent, you will take the full and whole responsibility of who you are, what you say, and what you do. That is why your viruses have to be handed out with happiness, reason, respect, and care.

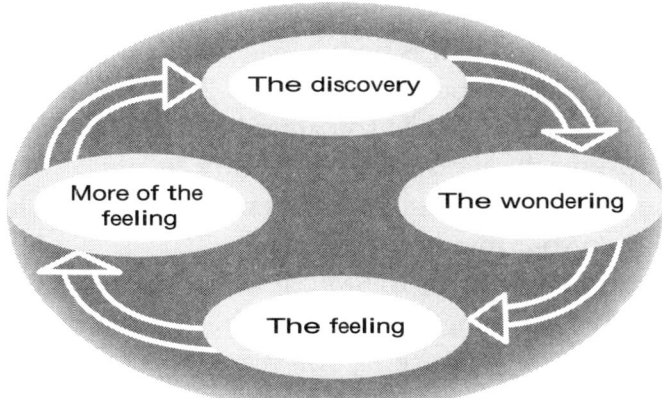

Source: Concept by author, drawn by Torunn Berg.

- You discover what it is you receive in life—some things that you have wished for and some things that you absolutely have not wished for.
- While you are wondering, you experience a conscious or unconscious feeling that is either positive or negative.
- The Law of Possibilities gives you more of that feeling.
- As a result, The Law of Possibilities gives you even more of that feeling and that is how the carousel starts spinning.

Now, the carousel starts spinning. At first it goes slowly, then a little bit faster and how fast it ends up going is all up to you. If the thought is positive and you want to relish in that feeling to the fullest and with deep breaths, you have to provide your carousel with nourishment so that it spins around faster and faster. The best part is when your carousel never stops spinning. Just make sure you always choose the right, positive thoughts so that your carousel increases its speed.

But it isn't always so. When negative thoughts arrive or you worry about something only you can understand, or that you maybe share with someone else, your carousel will spin just as fast, but this time it will be filled with negative energy. What is the purpose of that for you? Sometimes you will pull the brakes while you are riding the carousel filled with positive thoughts, slowing it down, eventually making it stop, and allowing other and less purposeful thoughts to sneak into your mind.

That's when it helps to be clear and concise to yourself. It starts by you being aware of what it is you radiate. If the frequencies are purposeful, you have to ensure that you encourage them even more, if not, you have to stop to make deliberate choices.

The Law of Possibilities always brings you more of the frequencies you already have, whether they are good or bad. The big question is: what do you want more of?

If you want to make changes in certain areas of your life, you have to make sure you change the frequencies of your thoughts.

The Three Steps of The Law of Possibilities

We are now going to have a closer look at the structure of the law. The law can be always used by anyone, and the more you use it, the more you will discover and become amazed by how it works.

What you put your focus on, bring energy to, and give your attention to becomes a reality whether you want it to or not.

It works every time. Sometimes right away, but at other times it may take days, months, or even years. It's all up to you. If you have big dreams, like the house of your dreams, for instance, you should not ignore that it might take years. But if you ever wonder whether or not your dream will become true, then just say "You just wait and see." When you salvage energies from your inner powers and know what it is you want, everything can be yours.

THE LAW IS VERY SIMPLE TO RELATE TO AND IS MADE UP OF THREE STEPS:

- Make your wish
- Increase the frequencies—believe it is possible
- Allow it to happen

So simple, but yet so hard. The law is short, simple, and easy to remember; however, it is also challenging. But, let's tread easily and have a closer look at each separate step to understand what it takes to make use of the law successfully.

The first thing you need to be aware of, or make a decision about, is what it is that you want, or what you are dreaming of, whether it is big or small.

Are you dreaming of bringing more fun and laughter into your life, or do you dream of writing a book? No dream is too big or too small, as long as it is your dream. Maybe the biggest challenge you might face is to really get to know yourself and what it is you actually do dream of? What do you dream of really? How aware are you of what it is you really want?

To make the law work in your favor, you have to be crystal clear. If you know your dream, write it down. Maybe your dreams are mundane, or maybe you wish to ride a hot air balloon, or even go all the way up to the moon? Don't limit yourself, but open up the top button of your shirt and allow your dreams to soar, without objections, not from yourself or from anyone else. To dream of a life without any constraints whatsoever feels fantastic and will be part of making the impossible possible.

Listen to Yourself

For you to be able to reach your dreams through using this law, it will be of the upmost importance that you listen to yourself instead of everybody else. Listening to yourself to figure out your own wishes and needs might be a challenge in itself, especially if you haven't already been in touch with your dreams. Concurrently, your ability to listen to yourself will be absolutely essential, and the most vital thing you need to do is to be able to live a life that feels meaningful, important, and valuable to you.

Listening is closely linked to communicating. Right now you might be reading this book because you want to get in touch with, or understand how to get in touch with, the contents of the life you are dreaming of. The challenge might be to figure out what it is you need to do or change to get started.

Reading, writing, talking, and listening are the four basic forms of communication. You are surely employing one or more of them quite actively. If I dare to challenge you a little bit, then I will claim that listening is the form of communication you are utilizing the least—listening to yourself and to others. Your ability to make good use of all the different forms of communication will be essential for what it is you will be able to attain and essential for what you will be able to accomplish by making use of The Law of Possibilities.

So how about a small challenge: you have spent years learning to read and write. You have spent and do spend lots of time talking. But what about listening? How many hours of training have you spent really listening to yourself, or others, that has resulted in a real and deep understanding of what has been thought or said? Lots of people have not had any practice with listening at all.

For you to really understand yourself, or others, you need to listen more. You might claim that you do care and value yourself, and that you do believe that you are a good listener.

But how can you be in touch with your own values if you haven't really listened to what they are? Or maybe you actually have listened to them, but have spent all of your energy fitting them into your surroundings? Maybe you have focused solely on the words. Your subconsciousness doesn't believe just the words; it values your feelings for the situation better. Technical words don't quite cut it. It takes feelings to make it real.

At First, Try to Understand, Then, Try Being Understood

The human being is an odd creature that typically finds it easier to try being understood. Maybe you too are one of those who does not listen enough to understand, but just to figure out how you are to reply when it is your turn to speak. This is where your self-conversations come in, the conversations that you have with yourself, in your mind, the conversation you hold with your inner landscape, that only you can hear, where you always find your own answers to your own thoughts, which, according to your own consciousness, are always right. That's where you are running your own movies and see them through your own glasses. And that's where you will find your own truth, which might be very different than your reality.

I found this charming example that I want to share with you, because I caught myself smiling when the last sentence revealed itself. It is about a father telling a friend how his son does not understand him. The friend is trying to understand what the father is really trying to say and repeats: "Is it so that you do not understand your son because he does not want to listen to you?" The father nods in agreement, acknowledging that that's how it is. Then the friend makes the comment that I find very profound: "But I thought understanding another human being was all about listening to him."

The father continues his reasoning, admittedly stopping for a moment, but after a short while he continues by saying that of course he understands his son and what it is that he is going through. After all, he'd been through the same things, in similar situations. But still, he could not understand why his son wouldn't listen to him.

What the father obviously does not comprehend is that what he is doing is to solely picture things in his head. He is running his movie and thinks that he can see what's going on in the world, including his son. But the father doesn't really have a clue about what is really going on inside his son's head. Can you see it? It is an obvious example of a person that has very little experience in listening.

I have had similar experiences myself. Facing challenges makes people want to help you. Everybody is not alike, but most people think in the same manner as the father of my little story.

Another small example from my own daily grind can be part of confirming this story too. Despite the fact that it was us that had to deal with challenges, there were lots of people around us who willingly shared their worries about us—as if we didn't have enough to deal with already with our own worries! Or because they wanted to give us advice, they started out by saying, and I can't even think any poorer way of starting a sentence than one that starts with: "Isn't it just too ..." or "If I was you, I'd ...." These are statements that disclose that person's own movie of life. Well put. Sure, but for whom? Personally, I think it is well put for themselves. Their suggested solutions harmonies with that person's own movie, and additionally, it gives them the feeling of being the "good little helper." My advice for you in similar situations would be: ask first, figure out what it is the person needs help with, and then, afterward, share yourself.

A person facing challenges and one who doesn't live in two different worlds. What's needed is that you first listen, understand, and then help. The next time you meet someone who has to make choices to overcome difficult situations, you should know that the best thing you can do is to ask them the following question:

How do you need me?
Or: Who can I be for you, in the situation you are in now?

That's when you are a good listener and helper, without you running your own show. Only then you will dare to open up to understanding the other one and will be able to help with the other ones needs. Then you will surpass whatever feels right for you. Then you will be a good listener, not a "talker." That's when you are a good helper.

Just like this, it will be important for you to listen to your own inner voice to be able to succeed with The Law of Possibilities. Be engaged in yourself, listen, and get a feel for what it is you want to achieve or what it is you need. The law will give you what it is you wish for, but only when you transmit tangible and solid wishes.

Listen to the silence, it can tell it all.

—Susan Jeffers

At this first stage, it is the words that are important and I strongly recommend that you write down your dreams. Then you will see them and they will appear in front of you with much more clarity—as a great tool for you to communicate with yourself.

When we talk, we use words—we read them, we write them, we hear them, we think them, and we see them. The words you see, that carry your dreams within them, will radiate your dreams in an important way for you. That's why I'll say it again: write your dreams out—and later in this book, you will gain more insight into why.

All words contain frequencies. Words such as "don't do it," "don't," and "no" also have frequencies, but as you might already be thinking, those frequencies are negative. To be able to find a way of writing down your dreams, it is important for you to create a setting that you enjoy, a setting that inspires you to really make time for your dreams. In my world, I call it "time for important meetings" with myself. It is all about you making an appointment with the most important person in your life, yourself. You have to schedule in an appointment with yourself, including both a date and a specific time—believe it or not, that's how specific you have to dare to be. This might be your first challenge. Overbooking could be very easy at this stage, allowing appointments with others to become a higher priority—because the appointment with yourself can just be postponed a little, right. If you do, you are not as ready as you thought. Because the events of life happen when they are supposed to, just like The Law of Possibilities do too.

I will encourage you to keep your own appointment. You don't even have to tell anyone about it, you can simply say: "Sorry, I'm busy then, but maybe we can arrange it for another time?" If you want something bad enough, you will always find the time for it.

When you are about to take on The Law of Possibilities, it will be an experience in itself to create an atmosphere around yourself that you will enjoy, a place you feel good to be in. Find the nicest room in the house or in the apartment you live in. Close the door, light lots of candles, if you have a fireplace, light it, and possibly even pour yourself a drink. Get out large pieces of paper and lots of colorful crayons or pens so that you can write out or draw out your dreams on the paper. Another variation would be to cut out pictures from magazines that harmonize with your dreams, even your computer will do to help you visualize your dreams. Test it and find the tool that works best for you. Knowing that what you see, the visual aspect of it, accounts for about 80 percent of the impressions that affect you, then you will understand why paper, pens, scissors, glue, or a computer screen are so important.

Now you are getting somewhere. Also, remember to turn off your mobile phone, as well as any other disturbing elements, disconnect your doorbell, and turn off your radio. Now it is all about you and your thoughts and the wonderful silence that will bring you where you want to be. Some light music without lyrics can provide you with that light touch of background music you might not be able to be without. Just make sure you are in a comfortable environment, that is, after all, the most important.

Now, you are really doing it and it feels good, doesn't it? Spend some time, play a little bit, enjoy yourself through this process, and devote as much time to it as you need. It doesn't even matter if you use several days.

The best part is that you have made a decision to start. That's the first step of your journey to the future you are dreaming of.

> *You cannot change worries and problems flying like birds above your head. But you can stop them from building nests in your hair.*
>
> —Chinese saying

How to Make The Law of Possibilities Work?

Step 1

Make Your Wish

Your dream can include every aspect of your life: career, money, your choice of partner, friends and friendship, business relations, education, or lots and lots more. The only limitation will be your fantasy and your decisiveness. You should know that people are very quick to make decisions regarding smells, sounds, and tastes. On the other hand, when it comes to relations, money, and career decisions, it is exactly the opposite. In these areas of life, people tend to need lots of time, sometimes they take too long, and sometimes decisions aren't even made at all.

Do you know what it is you want? Do you know that you are the only one creating your life? Can you feel your wishes pulsating within you? Or are you like most others who don't really know? Maybe you have even stopped believing that it will be possible for your dreams to ever come true?

Know that there is nothing you cannot do, no one you cannot be, or nothing you cannot get as soon as you master the three steps of The Law of Possibilities. Right now, we're only doing the first step of the law. But maybe it has already crossed your mind that it can challenge you into figuring out what it is you want?

One way of becoming aware of what you want is to start by asking yourself: what is it that I don't want and what is it that I don't want more of? What is it that does not feel good in my life or puts me in a negative state of mind? What is it that leaves worry-viruses in my life right now?

Often it is easier to discover what it is you really want and what possibilities you have if you, at first, understand what it is you don't want or what it is that worries you. Or to say it another way, it can be vital to observe your worries, because they will help you in seeing your possibilities.

Take out a pencil and piece of paper and divide the paper into two columns with a straight line. On the left side of the paper, you are to write down all of your worry-viruses.

Below you will find help in the form of a few examples of possible worry-viruses gathered from a list made by one of the clients that I have worked with.

WORRY-VIRUSES	POSSIBILITY-VIRUSES
• I feel despair and insecurity when facing new situations.	
• I feel despair when I do not feel up to the challenge.	
• I feel a sense of dissatisfaction with myself when meeting friends/colleagues that I think dress well and look good.	
• I suppress myself when people around me emphasize themselves and their abilities.	
• I think my education is insufficient.	
• I focus on the things at work that irritate me and stress me out.	
• My head is filled with thoughts of how nothing feels good enough, right here and now, and that somewhere out there, there is something so much better.	

All of these statements tell us something about what she dislikes and what she worries about in the situation she is in. The statements represent areas of her life that she absolutely does not want more of or that she wishes were different.

That's how you too can deal with negative sentences that bring negative vibes when they come and disturb your inner landscape and turn them into sentences that start with "in the past" or "before."

Here Are Some Examples of How Some of the Worries Can be Turned Around:

- Before, I felt despair and insecurity when facing new situations.
- Before, I could not help suppressing myself.
- In the past, I put too much focus on the things that irritated me and stressed me out.

The key is to put the words before or in the past in front of the worrisome sentences.

Other worry-viruses that you could be putting too much emphasis on are that you never will find the right boyfriend or girlfriend, that you never will be able to quit smoking, that you are groaning in dissatisfaction over the fact that your postbox is seemingly bursting its seams from all of the bills that keeps coming into it, or that you are not enjoying your work—these are just to give you a few examples. As you see, there are lots of different areas in life that make people worry. That's why it is all about you increasing your awareness of your own grounds. What you will discover is that most worries turn into nothing and you will realize that most worries are just momentary and will pass. In the end, they are, or will be, important sources of learning.

When you have completed the left column of your paper with your worry-viruses, the time has come for the part of The Law of Possibilities that will be much more enjoyable to work with. Now, you are going to be turning your worries around so that based on them, you will be able to see the opportunities laying ahead for you. Now you have taken the first significant step into the journey to the future, where you will always get what you want! Just because The Law of Possibilities gives you more of the things you radiate, it is so important for you to quickly remove your attention from the things you don't want and toward the things you really do want. That way you can really notice all of the fantastic opportunities available for you. The key to achieving what you really want, without being stuck in your old ways and the things you don't want, is to truly pay attention to what it is that you have written.

Now the time has come to turn the negative into something positive. Let's go back to the statements in the previous example to see what they would look like in a positive version.

Most of the properties and chemistry of the possibility-viruses are all about changing your thoughts and statements. If we were to rephrase the negative frequencies in our example, then the possibility-viruses could be something like this:

WORRY-VIRUSES	POSSIBILITY-VIRUSES
- ~~I feel despair and insecurity when facing new situations.~~	- I always feel safe and secure when facing new situations.
- ~~I feel despair when I do not feel up to the challenge.~~	- I am capable of dealing with all kinds of challenges and situations.
- ~~I feel a sense of dissatisfaction with myself when meeting friends/ colleagues that I think dress well and look good.~~	- I am thoughtful and kind. I am cheerful and I create happiness and laughter in my life. I am a positive resource filled with luck.
- ~~I suppress myself when people around me emphasize themselves and their abilities.~~	- I am always sure of myself and enjoy being with other people that are "the life of the party."
- ~~I think my education is insufficient.~~	- I am skilled and possess a lot of knowledge.
- ~~I focus on the things at work that irritate me and stress me out.~~	- I focus on having pleasant conversations at work; I enjoy positive feedback and seek positive and happy environments.
- ~~My head is filled with thoughts of how nothing feels good enough, right here and now, and that somewhere out there, there is something so much better.~~	- I look forward to every new day.

Sentences written in the present tense, that is, statements phrased in the now, make all of the difference. That makes the message obvious and crystal clear. Something else that might be worthwhile for you, in the process you are in right now, is to "rid yourself of" your worries by physically removing the worry part from your sheet of paper. Cut it and throw it away, or just simply fold the paper over so that you can no longer see your worries in print anymore. Some people might need to go as far as to throw their worries in a bin bag, carry the bin bag out of their house, and put them in the bin to be able to reach the good feeling of finally getting rid of their worries once and for all. Do what you feel you need to do.

If you are still wondering whether you are projecting positive or negative radiation toward certain areas of your life, simply check into that specific area and see what it is you receive. Is it a perfect match? Are you really getting what you want? Again it can be smart to realize that:

What you give of yourself is what you get back.

How much time are you going to spend on this part of the process? That's all up to you. Some will need lots of time, maybe a week, while some only need a day. Only you can decide how much time you will need, but the most important is taking the time and allowing yourself all the time you need. In some instances, we can reach our decisions quickly, but with others we just need more time. Now, you have a tool that can help you in becoming aware of what it is that hinders you from reaching your dreams.

Step 2

Increase the Frequencies—Believe it is Possible

This step is all about increasing your frequencies. Boost the intensity of the possibility-virus, let all the "germs" loose, and let them get in the game for all it is worth. Make sure you become contaminated to the point that it makes your entire body bubble and gurgle.

Everything that you direct your attention to starts frequencies. The frequencies you emit are the ones that will bring your response back too. Equal attracts equal. So if there is something you want that you haven't yet received, you now know what to do. One word of caution: avoid focusing all of your attention to the things you don't have because the way the law works is that then it will still be lacking—you'll just get more of it, namely lack.

Think of your feelings being like a roller-coaster or a carousel. You get in, and the carousel starts spinning faster and faster. You rejoice in the speed, your stomach tickles, and you feel real, childlike sensations of happiness. It can be just like that with how you nourish your dreams or the goal you have set out to achieve too.

If you feel just a tad of frustration or disappointment because your dreams aren't coming to you as quickly as you had expected—maybe you're even wondering if your dreams will ever come true—before you pick yourself up again and move on. This situation can simply be compared to you trying to reduce the speed of your carousel: just like when you are putting your foot to the ground, scrubbing it to slow the carousel down; it still spins, but you no longer feel that childish exhilaration for the momentum and the delightful ticklishness in your stomach slowly withers away.

And if you become negative, it will be like the carousel plunges to a halt and stops completely. It does not spin anymore: there is no speed and little or no joy at all.

With this metaphor, you can make a discovery of your own daily routine and what your thoughts and feelings do to you.

Identify the things that make you feel good and make your carousel spin with the delightful pace you feel is right for you and simply start doing more of them.

Now that you understand that you yourself are frequencies that also contain feelings, it will be easier for you to create your reality in a more conscious manner. You can be, do, or get everything you wish for because you are energy, awareness, and frequency. This might all sound kind of odd in the beginning, but it will be useful for you to start accepting the fact that it is your thoughts that create frequencies, which connect with your feelings and generate your experiences. When you reach an understanding of the way your experiences happen, then the mystery and your skepticism will swiftly be replaced by possibility-thinking, learning, and a lot of personal growth.

Think of it as all your frequencies create your destiny and that is why it will be so important for you to make your decisions based on what you feel is right for you. Don't make decisions based on what you think you have to do, or what is expected of you, if that makes you feel like it creates some kind of resistance or conflicts within yourself. I will come back to this later in the book.

> *Your frequencies and what you believe in have to match for you to get what you want.*

Practice, Practice, Practice

To be able to reach this feeling, it will be necessary to "practice." Everybody knows what going hiking in the woods or working out in a gym is like, but how often do you practice living life itself?

It starts when you make yourself aware, catch yourself in your own frequencies, and make sure your focus is in the right place, depending on what situation you have found yourself in. Negative frequencies need to be transformed, and positive frequencies must be repeated and practiced.

This is hysterically funny and fantastically exciting. It will bubble and tingle when the positive frequencies are let loose within your body—it will feel like it is your birthday and Christmas all at once. The difference is that it is you that has made the present for yourself, and that everything is happening inside the gift wrapping, that is, within your own body. It is yourself and your body that you are presenting for everybody else to see. What is happening on the inside is your own secret and possibility all at the same time. It is your thoughts, your feelings, or the conversations that you carry on with yourself that nobody else can hear. In there, you will find the questions and the answers you generate yourself, where you have stored everything you can and feel, and where you feel what is happening to you when you receive outside influences.

Your inner self is only yours. You're the boss, you're the one making the choices, and you're the one calling the shots. In there, it is all up to you how it fluctuates. It is from within there you find your power, no matter what is going on in your life. It is from within there, you will really get in touch with your true potential.

The best way to start positive frequencies and to nurture the possibility-virus is to find out what it is that feels good— and to do more of it. You just simply have to work out your own strategy of how to feel good. It's the feeling that counts. And you will come to understand that the meaning of life is to feel and experience absolute and complete happiness.

What is it that Makes the Results?

As the curious possibility-agent you are about to become, you have probably snooped, poked, and pried into at the fact that it is the feelings that are pivotal—what you feel inside of you—and not just the plain words. But it starts with the words, so the words do count too.

> **SOME IMPORTANT SENTENCES ON THE ROAD TO ACHIEVING RESULTS ARE:**
> - I am about to attract ...
> - I am in the process of attracting ...
> - I have decided to ... or
> - A lot can happen when ...

Even sentences that start with: I hope that ... will be significant because you do admit to allowing a little bit of something to happen, but that you will still need more energy.

While the possibility-agents are fully convinced that the law is really amazing and that no matter what, it always works, you might still need some more help with the words that will bring you further along on your journey of curiosity. The alternative is for you to open up and tell yourself that your job now is to make The Law of Possibilities work for you.

Use Wishful Sentences

Wishful sentences will help you to form good sentences that lead you toward wonderful frequency-possibilities. Here are some examples of how you can start those sentences. Fill in with your own dreams and wishes:

- I love knowing that my dreams are ...
- I love the feeling when ...
- I have decided to ...
- More and more comes my way in regard to ...
- It makes me happy to know ...
- I am thrilled over the thought of ...

The secret is that all of these words are words that express feelings. We don't dedicate enough attention to our feelings. Our feelings are our most important antennas to this magnificent life of wearing loose-fitting clothes every day, rather than tight-fitting corsets all the time. All humans have feelings, there's not a soul that doesn't have them, but we all may find it much too easy to ignore them.

These wishful sentences are very valuable because they increase your frequencies slowly, but surely and they send important messages to your subconsciousness. Wishful sentences are a much more effective tool rather than, for example, affirmations, which for many doesn't seem to work as well. The reason for this is that affirmations are mostly words, but The Law of Possibilities not only responds to words but also the feelings you associate with these words as well. If you look at yourself in the mirror every morning just after getting out of bed, with an affirmation saying: "I look fantastic," but yet you feel what you're seeing absolutely does not match with the words you are using, then The Law of Possibilities is so distinct that it will even give you more of what you don't want.

What you might be seeing is a tired, colorless face that does not feel very much like a fantastic edition of yourself. Then it might be very helpful to have a wishful sentence that goes something like this: "I love the feeling of looking fantastic." Simple, positive, enriching, and powerful.

Honesty and love are important prerequisites to be able to perform. It starts with being honest with yourself. If you are honest with yourself, you will appear honest to others. You will be comfortable with yourself and others will be comfortable with you as well. You won't have to let others think they know you. Together with the valuable insight this brings, your feelings will also naturally fall into place. Even intuition will become a natural part of your life.

Intuition is nothing but a feeling you get or have in a specific situation that cannot be explained. This feeling appears and disappears quickly, so it is imperative to take notice of it as it emerges and to act according to it. This feeling is real, it is all yours, and it will always bring with it something of value to you. Both men and women have intuition. Maybe you need to start discovering it and start to take notice of what your intuition is trying to tell you. It always has a message for you, and it is incredibly valuable. Your intuition will put you in touch with unimagined possibilities and experiences, which in turn will give you the opportunity to understand yourself and your surroundings better and to understand others. These possibilities can help you act in ways that ultimately also will bring you more happiness, success, and well-being. If you want to have more intuition in your life, all there is to do is to get a grip on it. Make a decision of something you want to achieve, create the right attitude, and boost your consciousness.

If you have doubts, you can challenge your doubt, and play and educate yourself to new insights. Have faith in knowledge, keep learning, continue filling your brain with more information, but challenge yourself to educate yourself in several ways. Life is so much, much more than what is found between the covers of a book or what other people tell you.

Can you remember back to the days you learned to walk, learned to ride a bicycle, solved the mysteries of skiing, or learned to dance? Did you read it in a book? Hardly. You learned it by doing it—and by doing it over and over and over again, until you've mastered it. And as if that wasn't enough, you even had an entire cheerleading squad around you, clapping their hands, and cheering you on: "Come on, you almost made it, try once more, give it another shot, yeah, that's great, you did it!" You were surrounded by lots of laughter, smiles, and happiness. This cheerleading squad might not be there in your life now, if you have become an adult, but then you have to become your own cheerleader! Encourage yourself, tell yourself how good you are, and tell yourself that you can make it: I am basically good, and there is basically a lot of things that I am pretty good at. Conversations with yourself can be useful in this way too. Another alternative is to ally yourself with a possibility-agent that you can share your joys with, that you can get to become your cheerleading squad when you need more than yourself to continue educating and growing. Because there are only possibilities that exist, right?

Now you have become acquainted with the first two steps of The Law of Possibilities. You might have already decided on what it is you want out of life, and you might even already be practicing, on a daily basis, how to increase the positive frequencies. Because you don't want more negative influences, do you? Then there's only the third and last step left.

What I wish for you is that you now have acquired an understanding of, through your new insights, that where you are in life right now and what you experience is very dependent on the frequencies that you have radiated, consciously or unconsciously.

Step 3

Allow it to Happen

Allowing it to happen simply implies not having any doubts. This step is the most important, but also the most challenging, for most. It's all about allowing yourself to receive what you are asking for. Because if you're not willing to accept all of the fantastic things you're asking for, it will seem like your questions aren't answered, even though they, in fact, are. It is connected with the fact that your frequencies do not match up with your wishes, and thus they simply won't let them in.

Where Does the Doubt Come from?

The most common source of doubt is our own limiting system of belief, which are your own thoughts of yourself, or what the conversations you carry on with yourself really tell you. For instance, have a look at the famous saying: "You won't achieve anything without hard work." It directs your attention toward and brings vibes of inadequacy and shortcomings, which in turn will prevent you from reaching your goal.

> **LET'S HAVE A LOOK AT SOME EXAMPLES OF WORRY-VIRUSES:**
> - I cannot do it.
> - It is so hard.
> - I really don't deserve it.
> - I will never make it.
> - Everyone else has got it, just not me.
> - If I ever could go that far.
> - I wish it was me.

But the fantastic part about thoughts is that they can be changed.

The response rate of The Law of Possibilities, that is, the velocity of your frequencies is connected to how much you allow things to happen.

Telling yourself that you don't have any doubts won't make the opportunities come by themselves, there's got to be more to it. Everything has two sides to it: what you want and the lack of it. Simultaneously, you are, as a human being, put together in such an odd manner that you might believe that you do have the right focus all of the time, but in reality, you're actually focusing on the opposite of what you want.

HERE ARE SOME EXAMPLES THAT MIGHT MAKE IT EASIER TO UNDERSTAND THIS:	
• I want to attract the perfect job	**Possibility-virus**
• I don't want my present job	Worry-virus
• I want to stay healthy	**Possibility-virus**
• I don't want to get sick	Worry-virus
• I want to be financially independent	**Possibility-virus**
• I don't want to experience not having enough money	Worry-virus

As you see, the word "don't" is worthwhile to skip, and it will be smart to be a little bit more conscious of your thoughts. You have to keep your focus on your wish, not the lack of it. That's when you'll be a proper possibility-agent. The creative powers work whether you are aware of it or not. If you're not mindful of it and keep your focus on the things you don't want, your wishes cannot come to you.

That's why your life will become so much more exciting if you consciously compare your thoughts with what is happening to you in your life. The wonderful day of celebration will be the day you understand your feelings and the important message they have for you. The day you let your feelings become in charge, that's the day you know where you are headed in life.

That's why it is so important for you to understand what is implied by allowing. Just having a strong wish and increasing the frequencies aren't enough. It is only when your doubts are completely gone that your wishes will manifest themselves. The faster you remove your doubts, the faster your wishes can become a reality too.

Imagine yourself getting into your car to drive from Boston to New York. You have made arrangements with friends you haven't seen for a long time. You're going to a concert and you have to be there at a certain time. You are really looking forward to this, it's the first time you are bringing your sweetheart and your car is brand new—your dream car. The gas tank is full and you are ready to go, the journey can begin. You have checked the map, chosen the best route, and you are on your way. You are driving through beautiful scenery with your honey by your side, so consumed by the wonderful atmosphere and your anticipations that you completely forget to keep an eye on the fuel gauge. In the middle of nowhere, you run out of gas and there's not a gas station for miles and miles around. Now you are faced with some choices of reaction.

You may feel so stupid and despaired that it knocks the wind out of you. You might put your head in your hands not knowing what on earth you are going to do. The thought you are thinking is that you'll never make it to New York, that's for sure. You have no confidence in getting there.

Another way you can react is that: ok—in this situation you need to get another car to pull over and give you a lift to the nearest gas station, so you can buy a spare can, fill it up with fuel, and get back to your car. Or maybe you could even get someone to tow you to the nearest fuel station?

Regardless, you have learned something important and you still have confidence in that you will make it to New York. You'll get there later than planned, you might miss parts of the concert, but you will get there.

The last reaction, which is in line with The Law of Possibilities, is to make yourself focus and pay attention to the fuel gauge as you go. Filling the tank at regular and frequent intervals, making sure you do have enough petrol, giving you unconditional confidence in arriving in New York at the right time. And you will too.

THE POWER OF ALLOWING IS IN THE PROCESS:

- Having a powerful dream along with strong doubts will make your wishes stick.
- Having a powerful dream along with some doubts will lead to you achieving your wishes even though it will be at a slower pace.
- Having a powerful dream without any doubts will make your wishes come true faster than you ever imagined, even possibly taking your breath away.

It is the power within the thoughts that makes things happen. If your thoughts are positive, it will happen, just like negative thinking will lead to the opposite. Being stuck in the negative is not really very worthwhile.

The negative in life punishes you and the positive rewards you, so here you just have to make choices again. Life is filled with situations in which you have to make choices. During the course of just one day you will make choices, even up to several ones. Like a politician, you too will go to election. The difference is that you will go to election on your life and that you, unlike the politician, will have to live with all the choices you make. So make sure that you create a fantastic party policy, a policy that will ensure that you win the election every time.

Every time you make a choice, you change the future—magnificently and fantastically. Give it some thought here and now. Give these words a bit of your attention, and deposit them into your "training account." Know that the most hopeless of situations can be turned around into the most tremendous opportunity by thinking positive thoughts about it. Your feelings are like the radar that always lets you know with which degree you allow or resist a connection. As you consciously study yourself and your feelings, you will become better at controlling the energy and to become a happy, conscious creator of your own life.

Now you really know all there is to know to get more of the things you want in your life.

How fast The Law of Possibilities will work is directly proportionate with how much you allow to happen.

Even a road thousands of miles long starts with a single step.

—*Japanese words of wisdom*

A Few Words about Confidence

Confidence is the highest form of human motivation, and it brings out the very best within people. Attaining confidence takes time, and patience and practice is of course important. People who believe that it is impossible to have confidence and trust in others may have grown up without good role models or have encountered situations that have brought them inappropriate experiences. If the contact with your own potential and positive active thoughts is absent, then active mental training will be worthwhile to find back your confidence in yourself and in others.

All people have the ability to develop. Personal development is really a continuous process that never stops and it is up to you whether you want to push this process on. Everything in life is up to you, including the unconscious or the conscious thoughts you have and what kind of attitude you have.

HERE ARE SOME EXAMPLES OF POSITIVE, ACTIVE THOUGHTS THAT MIGHT BE AN INSPIRATION TO YOU:
- Lots of people can do what I dream of every day.
- Very much in life is easy and straightforward.
- I deserve the best in the world.
- Everything is possible.
- Some people have what I dream of right now.
- I can also reach that far, lots of people have done it before me.
- I look forward to it becoming my turn.

Here and now, I challenge you to start somewhere.

There are no shortcuts to any place worth going.
—Beverly Sills

Who Can Become a Possibility-agent?

Absolutely, anyone can become a possibility-agent and for the first time you will be rewarded for recruiting new agents. Because every human being acting as possibility-agent, contaminating the world with possibility-viruses, will be part of making the world a better place to be. You will be doing something great and fabulous for the planet we live on and for the times we live in.

As a Possibility-agent, You Can Make:

- More people smile a whole lot more.
- More reporters write about positive events and incidents because that is important news.
- The children at school play more, because the teachers will see the value of playing.
- The church become more alive and accessible for everyone.
- People see the value of one another, regardless of race or skin color.
- Grown-ups play more and be less serious all of the time.
- The number of wars in the world reduce and make more room for peace.
- Power people let go more of their control.
- More people increase their focus on taking better care of the earth we live on.
- More people fully dare to be themselves.
- More people decide to do something rather than just going along with the masses.
- More people live according to The Law of Possibilities.

As a possibility-agent, you may have discovered, or you are about to discover, your own potential and how much easier it will be to live with the possibility-virus as your guiding light. You might have had to work with and practice a bit to reach the point where "possibility-thinking" is the fundamental value of your life and you may have found out how much easier your life has become due to positive frequencies. Perhaps you find your thoughts to be alternating and somewhat sporadic, entering but then withdrawing from this way of thinking, at where you are now, in this process. Know that life sometimes is a bumpy ride, and that you will always regain yourself from being down in the dumps. When you are down, you learn a lot, making your future depressions fewer and fewer. If you feel that you have become stuck in your inner conversation with yourself and find it hard—if you doubt whether the law really works because you don't see any result, just let it be. Accept that you're stuck, that it is ok, and that's where you are right now. What you will discover by accepting the situation is probably that your calmness and your collectedness will come back to you. Accepting a situation rather than pushing yourself on will give you a much more enhanced and quicker progress, once you are ready to move on again.

You might find it challenging to think of possibilities all of the time. That's just fine because you now know more about what it is you need to bring yourself back on track, back on the "road of possibilities" once again.

The possibility-virus is not just intended for the few, the selected ones. The possibility-virus makes the healthy healthier, the happy happier, the enthusiastic one even more enthusiastic. The possibility-virus is for everybody and does something for everyone.

Anyone can become a possibility-agent. Once you master The Law of Possibilities, you will be able to develop your potential into heights you never imagined possible. This just might be the last piece to fall into place in your puzzle in your life.

Ask and You Shall Receive

There are many people you can ask to help you achieve your dream or your goal. I can guarantee you though that it starts with you asking yourself about what your dream is and what it is you need to reach? Along the way, you might need to ask somebody else for help too to make things more clearly to you. Some will say yes and agree to help you, but others will say no and refuse. Just keep on asking, because quite possibly all you need is just one yes for you to attain what you really want. Something you shouldn't forget either is that there just might be someone out there simply waiting for your question. Today we do not have a culture that encourages asking for help, which prevents us from discovering what vast rewards can be found by simply asking someone for help. We have been raised in a way that is much more directed toward making it on your own, standing on your own two feet. Consider that most people are very often just waiting to be asked because one of the most important human core values is that we really do want to help. So do just like our precious and wise children, ask questions without any hesitation or reluctance.

Youthfulness is a matter of attitude, not about the year of birth.

—*Karl Lagerfeld*

How Do You Ask?

Ask for something like you already have what you wish for. Possibly, the most important reason for you to be asking for something is that you really want to attain what you are asking for, that you really believe in what you are saying or putting to paper. This is where senses come into play again. All people are capable of sensing whether someone is sincere and really believe in what they are asking for. What you radiate always reflects the assurance of your inner world. Your words reflect your inner beliefs, just like your body language, your eye contact as does the tone of your voice. Similarly, the things you put in writing will stand out, becoming much more apparent and distinctive for you.

For you to be completely on the ball with yourself—centered and balanced, when you ask for something, it could be of value to you to ask yourself some important questions:

- What would I be like if I knew for certain, 100 percent, that I would get exactly what I ask for?
- What would I say?
- What kind of body language would I make use of?
- What would I feel like if I was absolutely sure that I would get what I wanted?

When you ask for something like you already have it, you will ask with a positive anticipation. The Law of Possibilities will always be there to give you what you want when you think positive thoughts.

Dare to Ask for Help

There are so many amazing rewards out there waiting for you if you were to ask other people your questions when you can't find the answers yourself. Human nature is to want to help, and you don't have to do everything yourself because you are part of a larger community. With regard to favors, services, and things from other people, you have to be prepared for the fact that not everybody will be able to give you what you wish for. With The Law of Possibilities as your foundation, you will acquire everything you want, regardless, but first you have to know what to ask for. The very heart of every kind of progress and prosperity is: you have to "own" what you ask for, it has to come from the bottom of your heart with enthusiasm, and it has to be something that you are truly passionate about. Once you have found what it is you really want and dream of—then the focus, the energy, and the awareness that the law addresses through your words will become your next steps.

Humility and Gratitude

When you have practiced for a while and discovered the fabulous ways in which The Law of Opportunities works, when you start feeling friendly with the law and notice how your friendship is being returned, that's when the time has come to expel a large portion of humility.

Humility is, of course, important as you go through the entire process of working with, testing things out, and trying to get familiar with having the law as your companion. Still, being humble becomes increasingly important the further you and the law enter into a companionship. When you have reached the stage that resembles amazement, the stage where your attention to the law has become so high that you more or less consciously make use of the law on a day-to-day basis, it will be even more important for you to open the door to humility.

Why humility? Because the law will give you everything you ask for, big or small. At this stage, it will be essential to think through what it is you really are asking for. Humility is all about you showing gratitude and thankfulness for everything that comes your way, all the things that you have actually asked for or dreamt of. Most people associate dreams with something positive, and it is within this context you should exercise humility. You will come to discover that you will receive so much, but it will be crucial that you also have the ability to say those fabulous words: "thank you." These are words that I wish to hear more often in today's society, where we have access to absolutely everything.

You might want to be thankful for what you have received as negative experiences that you in fact have asked for too. That's when you really need to demonstrate what a magnanimous mind you have got, because the negative also comes into your path because you have asked for it. It might not always be easy to agree to this, since you never really wanted to be late for that train or loose the watch you inherited from your grandfather. You lost something, whatever it was, because you needed to learn something, or to help you choose a different direction or path. Go deep within yourself and find the sentence: "What is it that I am supposed to learn from this?" The funny part is that you will always get an answer. There will always be something that comes to you to give you new thoughts if you take the time to stop and listen.

There's learning incorporated in all situations of your life, whether the situation is positive or negative. But ask for the positive learning so that you rapidly switch back into having positive frequencies again. It is with positive radiation that life feels good to live. That's when we feel good with ourselves, and the world gives us a positive response back.

That's why humility is so important because you will actually get what it is you ask for, and it is important for you to be thankful for it. It isn't always necessary to be thankful toward another person; it is the situations where other people are involved you have to be thankful for. It will bring happiness to others and warmth to their souls in more ways than you can possibly imagine. Make sure you do more than just think that you want to say thank you, say it out "loud" so that everyone that deserves your thankfulness gets to hear it with their very own ears.

"Thank you" are such wonderful words that they deserve to be used a whole lot more in our society. You have endless things to be thankful for. If there is something you have achieved that only you know of, then at least say thank you to yourself. A little bit of personal care will do you so much good and you might even catch yourself smiling at yourself? And regardless, a smile is like balm for the soul. Thankfulness will bring with it so many new and great experiences.

I myself have a wonderful experience with regard to sharing my thankfulness. It all started with a meeting that I had one Monday morning. Later, when I was in my car and heading to the gym that's when I started my little séance of thankfulness. I sent out a thank you for the meeting I had just attended. I was thankful to be driving a warm car, for being able to put food on the table, for having a good and warm bed, a lovely family, and that I could work out in the middle of the day. And just like that, I went on and on and on. I parked my car and tossed my gym bag across my shoulder and headed into the fitness center. I had barely put my foot inside the door when one of the coaches said, "Wow—you look great today!" That was a very warm welcome, I thought to myself, before I thanked the coach for her very nice greeting. I headed toward the locker room, but before I even could put my hand on the door handle another coach came running over to me and said, "You are so beautiful today. Not that you aren't always beautiful, but today you are simply extraordinarily beautiful. I just had to say it, because I saw it the very instant you arrived." By now I almost felt a little bit uneasy, but even amazed and thankful too. So much attention in so little time! Simultaneously, I started to reflect over what it was that was different today. The answer had to be that the state of thankfulness I had been in and all of the thankfulness that I sent out before I got there must have done something to me and my radiance. My thankfulness had to somehow have materialized itself on me and become visible to everyone else. It all felt very magical and fantastically educational.

I will recommend to you and advise you to be thankful for everything the day has brought you, every evening before you go to bed. You can start by being thankful for 30 things that you feel thankful for today. The first time you do this exercise, 30 experiences may appear to be an enormous amount of experiences, but as you go along you will discover how much there really is for you to be thankful for—all "the trivialities"—that has happened during the course of the day. You can also be thankful for a new day filled with new possibilities.

Energy Bombs and Other Surprises

Everything is energy and all people are energy. It is the "energy edition" of people that I first and foremost want to put a little focus on and address right now. As the curious possibility-agent you are, or are about to become, you might encounter different challenges while starting to adopt the law, or even life in general for that matter. The biggest challenge you may come across will be the people you surround yourself with or the people you will meet on your new path of possibilities. Just like there are different flowers in nature, there are also different kinds of people. Some will be walking around, strutting their energy, having unfolded their petals, as the beautiful flowers they are in all their glory. Others won't have enough energy of their own and will be taking bits from anyone that is willing to give.

But energies are cunning stuff. Even though you will meet people strutting with energy, the energy could be either positive or negative, or a combination of both. And your energy will mix with the energy of other people as you are part of a community, which is life.

> *Every thought and every intention we radiate is energy. When you throw a rock in the ocean, the ripples will affect every atom of the ocean. When we put forward good intentions and thoughts toward others, we will have an effect on everybody around us and beyond.*
>
> —Unknown

The most important part is that you are aware of your own energy and take care of it and tend to it. All the time, you must work on staying within your valuable energy to protect it against energy thieves and readily leave situations that make you feel uncomfortable. Make sure to nurture your good and appropriate energy because first you need to be able to live well within your own energy and stand up to your own potential before you can give of yourself to others. That's why you will have more fun and live better when you are at one with yourself, when you know yourself, when you have a good connection with your own true self, feel content and happy with yourself, and that you treasure each and every single atom of your body, regardless and effortlessly. If you do, you can stand your ground no matter what hits you. You will be able to stand up for yourself, and you will be able stand up for others. That's why you are the most important person in your life.

Go in before you go out, get to know yourself before you find your spot in the outer, superficial world where things, symbols, and statuses easily become more important than who you really are. A genuine version of yourself will create real people around you and the energies will flow easily and effortlessly.

Doubters and Skeptics

There are skeptics everywhere and they will always be around. The skeptic is the one that limits their life to just those things they were taught in school or only to those things that can be found in the environment where they have gathered their references from. They are the one that has a conception of what they know is the only thing that's right. They have the conviction that you can only do things in certain predetermined ways. The one that never questions the established. The one that goes on autopilot every single day. The one that is afraid of a lot of things. The one that makes fun of others weaknesses, which in reality is just a mirror of themselves. The one that easily makes others laugh, but hardly knows how to laugh at themselves and at their own mistakes or screwups. The one that is just "visiting" here on earth and that may not live their life as a "whole" individual. The one that loves saying: "That's dangerous," and to them, everything is.

And while we're at it, please forget the saying you might have heard that the skeptic or the pessimist will always be right in the end.

They will never ever believe in The Law of Possibilities. They'll laugh at it and think: "What kind of crap is that—it surely won't work." But have they tried it? No. They simply don't have the faith, but then again, they don't even want it either.

You, though, who has started to become interested, you have got to enter your own "system of beliefs" and stay there. Just remain calm with your thoughts, try the law out, and play a little bit with it. Sometimes, it could even be smart not to tell the world all about what you are up to, until you have become fully acquainted and comfortable with The Law of Possibilities. As an alternative, you might want to spend time with other people that have discovered The Law of Possibilities too. Enjoy being together with other possibility-agents that also have discovered the possibility-virus.

To prevent your children from adopting this skeptical view of The Law of Possibilities, becoming negatively affected, it might be wise to tell them about your positive experiences with the law. Don't force it down their throats either, but let the children be naturally inquisitive and curious. Teach them that there is much more between the heavens and the earth than what can be logically explained. Let them be children for as long as possible, or rather make sure you always try to take care of the child within yourself. Childlike play is the best, even for grown-ups. Learn from the children because they have so very much to teach you, if you only allow yourself to be aware of it.

Incidentally, have you tried pulling a few pranks, or just being plain old silly, a little bit crazy, at a party, lately? I can guarantee that it will bring you attention and in addition you might even make other grown-ups around you laugh.

Believe me that won't be harmful at all. Laughing is healthy, it feels good, and it increases your levels of endorphins. You don't need a prescription and it even comes for free, no charge at all. Another way of looking at laughter and childishness is that they are simply other ways of improving your health. The skeptic, this doubting creature, will be more than happy to label you as a dupe, perhaps even call you childish and some of them might even think: "Oh my god, is it possible?" or "Imagine someone making such a fool out of themselves."

But just do it anyway, play and have fun. The result might be that you live happily and remain in good health for as long as you are here on earth. And you will be doing everyone a favour, even the skeptic, even though he or she has chosen a different attitude. It's his or hers, so let them keep it.

Laugh often and live longer.

The meaning of life is to feel complete and full of happiness. That's actually why we are here. Give it some thought, right here, right now, and decide what it is you believe in, what it is you want to be your faith.

The Envy-Virus and the Opposite

There is also an envy-virus that exists out there in our world. It has always been there, and it will quite surely always remain out there somewhere. Just make sure that you're not an envy-virus yourself. Envy is a very negative frequency that will only drain your energy. There is simply no positive purpose for envy at all.

Try to make your life into something bigger than yourself and do make use of all of your creativity and passion. All successful people have done what they love most of all and they have done it with their heart in it, with zest. Money has come to them as a result, as a bonus, but it has never been the goal of their success. Follow and pursue those things that spark your enthusiasm. Do things you like to do, things that you are good at, in fact, fantastically great at. Then there will not be any competition because it is the beauty within you that is the best part of your life. If you are to compete with someone then make sure it is yourself you are competing with. It is not necessarily all about being the biggest or the best, but being good enough. That will do in abundance, and it will give you the reward you might be searching for.

Possibility-rules

Since which edition of the possibility-virus you will receive is completely dependent on you, you have to make a decision whether you want more of the worries or if you want more of the possibilities. Increase your awareness and make active choices.

Be sure not to spread the worry-virus to others, if that's your choice. Also, make sure you do not open up to receive this negative virus from others.

Be Certain that You Have Permission Before You Contaminate Others

Take care that you do not overwhelm others with your belief in and your enthusiasm for the law. We are all at different stages in our lives. Some will become "infected" right away, others will need some more time before they discover how fantastic life can be lived with the law in their pocket, yet others won't even comprehend what on earth you are talking about and will call The Law of Possibilities a bunch of baloney. Willingly talk about the law to anyone you want to, but a good rule of thumb is to find out first whether the person you are talking to wants to become "infected." Ask for permission.

Even Ask For Permission When You Want to be Infected Yourself

You might run into people that have more experience in regard to using the law than you and that may make you want to have a refill, a new dose, of possibility-viruses. Then I will advise you to ask for it, or just open your senses and accept it and humbly receive from others that have something to teach you. Tell them that you want to become better. Perhaps you could start a group where you share experiences and, for instance, meet up with each other once a month. The Law of Possibilities is more about sharing than just giving and taking. Once you discover that sharing equals growing twice as fast, that's when life will open up to a whole new dimension, a whole new purpose. Don't sit around waiting for others to do something for you. Do it yourself.

Take Responsibility for What You Need

Often it will be tempting to make other people responsible for how we feel or what it is we experience. When things are uncomfortable or don't go our way, it is easy to think or say: "It wasn't my fault" or "Why did you have to do it like that?" Something that many people aren't aware of is that the errors and deficiencies they see in others often reflect what they need to learn about themselves. It could be, for example, something about their own insecurities, or their own way of dealing with things that happen.

If you use The Law of Possibilities and the positive frequencies, the chances are highly probable that you will get what you want. What is fantastic is that when you focus and think hard, your wish will materialize.

In addition, the more often you practice being in touch with what it is you have chosen to focus on, the better your chances are for it to come to you faster. A friend you see every now and then will get a hold of you faster because of your frequencies. The reason why that is you already have established a connection and over time you have nurtured it. The more you apply the law the more you make it yours and the faster the things you want will come to you. The experience of "being" the law will become a natural part of you.

The Reward

The Law of Possibilities isn't completely for free. The price you pay is the risk that you are involved with negative frequencies without being fully aware of what's going on so that you get more of the things you really do not want. Invest in your own positive effort, and The Law of Possibilities will give you your money's worth.

As children, we are naturally positive. We want to develop, we want to learn, and we want to grow as human beings. We are positively influenced by the people who love us and care for us. On the other hand, if we are influenced by negative people, or have parents that have negative frequencies as their natural behavior, we could develop a skeptical way of thinking.

If you have a conscious awareness of the positive, you will use the words: "You can cross the street when the light says Walk." Others would express exactly the same message just like this: "You cannot cross the street when the lights read. Don't walk." What they want to communicate is the same, but it is said with two distinctly different energies.

Possibility-agents can contribute to making you change your awareness and relieve the pain you carry with you in the baggage from your past. When we vibrate positivity, we confirm our wonderful experience of being a part of the world, we confirm our own growth and development, and we bring to mind all of the joy and the happiness that exist within us all. When we develop into more positive people, who see more opportunities in life than worries, we will discover all of the real, important riches within ourselves, which gives us more of what we are dreaming of and less of what we don't want. The price is quite reasonable and the reward isn't just great, it's amazing and incredibly huge.

Go Within Yourself Before You Go Out

Picture yourself having trouble with your eyes. You can't see as well as you used to and you decide to see an optician for help. After the optician has listened to your problems for a while, he takes his own glasses off and hands them over to you for you to try them. He's been using these glasses for five years and they have been a great help. It doesn't matter all that much for the optician to give you his glasses, after all, he's an optician and he can make himself as many pairs of glasses as he wants.

When you try them on you discover that it is simply worse, in fact, you can't see anything at all. The optician can't figure out what's wrong, because these glasses work just the way they are supposed to for him and he tells you to just try a little harder and to put some effort into it. Think positive is the piece of advice you are given. In your own opinion, you are being positive, but you still can't see a thing. Now the optician becomes irritated because he thinks he has done everything in the powers of his profession to help you.

The chances of you going back to this optician are fairly slim. You won't have much confidence and trust in an optician that doesn't figure out the problem with your eyes before he hands you his solution. Besides, his eye problems are hardly the same as yours. This goes for communication too, regardless of your form of communication. You can't make a diagnosis before you communicate. Again what is it you want? What is it you are dreaming of?

It is easy to end up in a superficial world trying to keep up with the Jones's rather than getting in touch with your inner wishes and needs. Like I have mentioned before, you were born free and unblemished of influences from others. As a child, you surely experienced being in touch with your own wishes and needs, but because you were dependent on adults, this could have turned out differently for everyone. But let me suppose that you did have an average and happy childhood, filled with play, laughter, happiness, and mastering with grown-ups as good supporters. Your grown-up cheerleading squad was there, helping you forward because they knew what you were good at—they saw your potential. They've had the same experiences in their past. If you think back and dig out your book of memories, then as a child you will probably recall your entire summer holidays as being filled with sunshine and beautiful weather throughout it all. Ok, maybe just once there was a short shower, but that's all. At this stage of your life you got to be just yourself, fully and in every respect, with your head, your heart, and your stomach. You thought, you sensed, and you felt, while there was always someone there for you to cheer you on, who made sure you reached your results successfully.

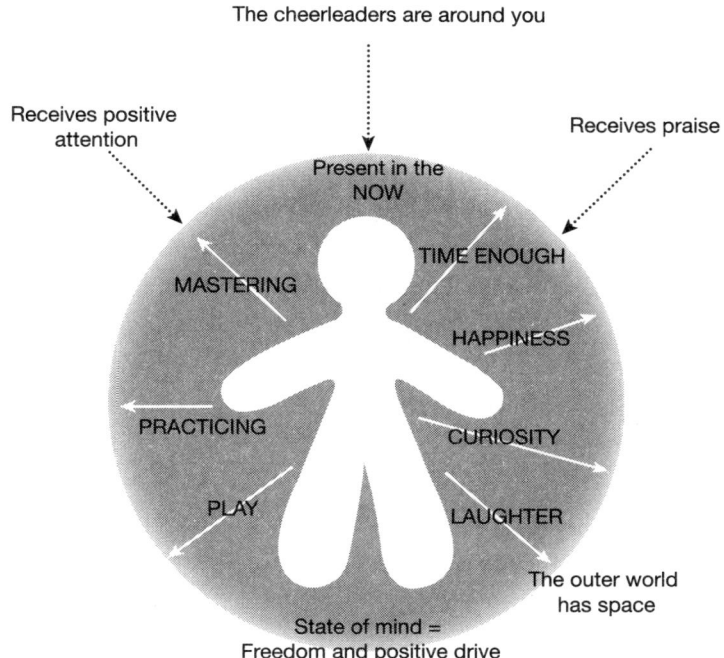

NORMALLY, CHILDREN ARE NATURALLY POWERFUL

Source: Concept by author, drawn by Torunn Berge.

But where is your cheerleading squad now? In your youth, or part of your adult life now?

Something happens along the way, something that makes you let go of your energy and travel further away from yourself. This is where The Law of Possibilities can come to your rescue and help you get back on track again. You have adapted to society and your surroundings, often at the expense of yourself and you slipped into a superficial world without bringing your own values along with you on your journey. Everything has happened gradually and over time without you even being aware of it. And additionally, maybe you did not even have good role models.

In the outer world, there are new factors that come in and take hold of your attention: responsibilities, school, work, associations, parents, commitments, things you "have" to do or "ought" to do, time, money, and even lots more. Within all of this there has to be space for yourself too. The big question has to be: what do you need to do to feel good about yourself and concurrently acting in line with your own needs? Again communication, listening to yourself, will become important. What language are you really using when you are talking with yourself, what's happening in your inner conversations, and what voice are you listening to?

The outer world pressing on

AWARE OF THE INNER CONVERSATION
KNOWLEDGE
RESPONSIBILITIES
TIME
ASSOCIATIONS
WORRIES
Present in
THE PAST – THE FUTURE
CAREER
SHOULD/OUGHT TO
CHORES
ADVERTISEMENTS
SCHOOL
TV
EXPECTATIONS
RULES
PRESSURE TO PERFORM
DEMANDS
IRRITATION
State of mind = Demands and tasks

ADULTS CAN BE FILLED WITH "ENERGY THIEVES"

Source: Concept by author, drawn by Torunn Berge.

NEGATIVE, PASSIVE LANGUAGE	POSITIVE, ACTIVE LANGUAGE
There's nothing I can do.	What alternatives do I have?
That's just the way it is.	I can approach this in a different way.
She makes me so mad!	I will take responsibility over my own feelings.
I have to do it.	I can choose another and more appropriate response.
I can't.	I can choose.
I have to.	I prefer.
If only ...	I want.

As you probably know, many of your experiences in life come from how you think and how you communicate with yourself. A negative, passive language is "It is not my responsibility"—controlled or put in another way: "I cannot choose the response"—controlled.

You choose how because you want the outcome of your choices. If you stay too long in a negative, passive language then it eventually will become a self-fulfilling prophecy and you will be searching for all the arguments you need to confirm that your way of thinking is right. You might even go so far as to blame the outer world, giving it the responsibility for the situation you're in, by attributing other people or circumstances the responsibility. In a world where you are the one disclaiming responsibility, The Law of Possibilities will be an interesting read because you will discover that equal attracts equal. You get more of what you are thinking of.

If your experience with the law is that it doesn't work on your first attempt, you might feel like dismissing The

Law of Possibilities as something silly that just some other foolish people do. But then, how are you really talking? Are you speaking in a negative, passive language or a positive, active language?

Life is all about loving yourself and others. For all positive, active people, the word "love" is associated with a deep feeling. These people are driven by the feeling of love. They turn love into a very great asset and can easily feel it. Love is an amazing asset that becomes active through loving actions and gestures. If you search for the positive in people, it will become much easier to find love and peace for yourself.

Become More Positively Active

One way of doing it is to have a closer look at how you focus your time and your energy. There are areas of your life that engage you: your health, your children, problems at work, or in other areas that only you know of. Within the areas that engage you, there are always areas that you can influence and there are circumstances or situations in which you have no influence. If you spend some time going over what it is you really do, use your time and energy at, you might reach some new and interesting realizations.

Positively active people spend their time and energy on areas where they can exert their influences. Like working with the things they can do something about. Then you will be working with and applying positive energies in areas in which you have influence, areas you can expand so that your total influence increases too.

Negatively active people focus on their concerns, for instance, other people's weaknesses. The things that exist in their surroundings that are creating problems and other things they can control. They have a negative language and an increasing feeling of being a victim. What these people have not thought of is that positive thinking can make them regain influence over their own life and that all the problems thus will diminish.

By working with self-development instead of worrying yourself sick over the circumstances, you will put yourself back in the driver's seat again. You will bring yourself further along the road where you can see that you have influence and which in turn will help you to grow and develop. It's you and only you, who are at the helm of your "ship."

Get a feel for whether you would like a situation in which you're in your own car. You are controlling the pedals while someone else is holding on to the steering wheel, choosing which way to go. If you want to be the one in charge of the steering wheel too, but feel that that's not how the situation is like in your life right now, it might be useful to change some of your habits. You could change some of the methods you use to gain influence over situations, or change the way you face situations where you do not have control.

They said it was impossible, so I gave it my best shot.

—Unknown

Possibility-possibilities

Now that you have become familiar with The Law of Possibilities, it is time for a peek behind the curtain and to receive some inspiration on how you can apply the law yourself.

*If you want to accomplish the goals of your life,
you have to begin with the spirit.*

—Oprah Winfrey

Senses and Feelings

For The Law of Possibilities to give you what you want, your senses are valuable tools and remedies. As you know, we have at least five senses. Here, we will concentrate on the five physical senses, those we register the outside world with and that makes us see, hear, smell, taste, and feel.

The registration, or the experience, is stored in your brain in the same location as the sense you used, when you had the experience and it is brought back again from the same spot. We can capture impressions from the world around us, bring back memories, and fantasize with all of our senses. Normally we obtain up to 80 percent of our information through our eyesight. As a result, a lot of us have found that good rules to remember are often based on pictures and images. A good runner-up is hearing.

It is fascinating, however, that even though the senses are different, they perceive your frequencies. And all of your senses take part in interpreting the challenges and gifts that life brings to you. That's why your feelings are important indicators of which frequencies you are in. When you discover which feelings you are in touch with, it will also be easier to discover which frequencies you respond with. Consequently, when you connect The Law of Possibilities together with the consciousness you experience while discovering something, you will get in touch with the frequencies you are setting in motion. And precisely here lies the valuable key to what you can get more of in your life. With this knowledge, you can route what you experience where you want it.

Your feelings are all about the connection you have with your natural powers and strengths, your inexhaustible source of energy, vitality, and vigor. Your emotions will fill you in on all of your questions and tell you everything you need to know about this source. Your feelings can most easily be compared with your true and veracious, ingeniously brilliant radar system. The emotions derive from the original thought you have started yourself, which gives you more of what you nourish through your thoughts. So when you do allow energy to emerge from your fabulous source of power, when you permit it to fully flow forward, then joy and happiness will fill your life.

You are free to choose your frequencies, so what is it you want more of? Every emotion belongs on a scale where happiness is at one end of it and hopelessness is at the other. When you then think thoughts that you feel are true to yourself, then happiness will freely flow throughout you. What can be better than to feel happiness, love, and freedom?

These are emotions you can feel every day by having a conscious focus. Feelings you may get more of through conscious training, when you write, listen, remain quiet, remember things, or visualize. In this manner, you can sense your way to happiness in your day-to-day life and in your life in general.

Take the Time to Cleanse Your Senses and Choose

Because our senses are our most important radar system, it is so that we also take in a lot of dirt too. We read bad news in newspapers and magazines, we absorb whatever the TV has to offer good or bad, and listen to mudslinging about other people. Or maybe we are part of the mudslinging? A quarrel or a heated discussion is as you now understand, frequencies too, and it is a part of what you have to relate to as a human being. It might be the frequency that you are radiating yourself, or you could end up in the same situation because of others. Again it is essential how you relate to these negative frequencies flowing through your senses and that you increase your awareness with regard to how you will refute the negative influences of your perception.

Your Senses Can be Cleansed

Through increased awareness, you will with practice discover when you are in situations with negative frequencies. Sometimes you can't get out of the situation right then and there, but you may be aware that it can be very worthwhile to cleanse your senses after such a situation. Don't try to analyze the situation, but as quickly as possible try to find something that brings you happiness. Search to find something that might give you a good laugh, the kind of laugh that comes from way down deep in your stomach, or anything it is that will give you a real and positive attitude. Maybe it is to paint a painting, listen to good music, or whatever it is that is your way of finding back to your positive frequencies as fast as possible.

Another alternative is to opt away from negative media influences by simply opting out of all the misery of the newspapers and magazines to look beyond the negative headline news stories and to look for the positive news that there well could be more of. For instance, you don't have to watch the evening news before you head for bed. You don't have to fill your senses with all of the tragedies of the world, bring them with you to bed to let them influence you throughout the night. If you've argued with your sweetheart you don't have to lie next to him, or her, in your queen size bed, but you can choose to go to sleep in another room just that night. Your subconsciousness doesn't sleep even though you do.

When you know that everything is energy, you can be focused and aware of who and what you associate with and what it is you want more of. If you've been in touch with negative frequencies, go to your positive sources as quickly as possible to get those inappropriate frequencies cleansed out of your system, get rid of them and move on. Switch on to positivity and get more of it. Equal attracts equal.

As you become conscious and fully aware of your feelings and your reactions, you will get better and better at managing your frequencies. With a little bit of discipline, you could become a conscious cocreator of more happiness in your life. It's not about controlling your thoughts, but rather managing them more consciously so that you experience more of what you want and less of what you don't want. The law and the conviction that it works will arrive through practicing it and experiencing with it. Again it is the power of the thoughts that makes things happen.

Visualization

Visualization is an effective technique for learning and change, a technique where you use your senses to create the results you want. The purpose of visualization is to activate your subconsciousness and to get your right brain half to contribute with its creativity. The areas of application will typically be to let the subconsciousness work on creative input and suggestions while giving the brain peace and quietness to think things through in an alpha wave condition. This is the ideal learning condition, a condition that's called "relaxed concentration." Many people will experience this as a semidrowsy state of mind and believe that their concentration and ability to learn is reduced. But that's not the case. However, if you are too exhausted, then your thoughts will quickly slip into the theta state (drowsiness) and then into the delta state (deep sleep). On the other hand, if you are too focused on a problem or a specific objective, your brain will be functioning at the beta level (conscious focus). At the alpha level, you will be in a condition right in between, a sort of meditative condition, where your mind can gather conscious thoughts together with unconscious information to create something entirely new. At this state of mind, information flows freely between the two halves of the brain. Fantasy, imagination, and creativity are released, and this condition contributes to inspiration, faster learning, and better memory.

Through the images at the alpha level, you can create anything, fantasize, and see before yourself at what it is you are dreaming of: a deserted island only for you and your sweetheart, yourself on top of the mountain you always have dreamed of climbing, a slimmer version of yourself, yourself in an airy parachute, or bungee jump, yourself dancing with joy all over the living room floor, singing in a choir, in your dream job, and just like this, you can go on and on indefinitely. It is only your own imagination that sets the limits. Create an image in your mind where you can see yourself in the surroundings that are the arena of your dreams and please include as many details as you possibly can.

Is there anybody else but you there? What colors do you see? Lights—darkness—scents—sounds? Use all of your senses. While visualizing you can really be playful with your senses. The combination of visualizing and using more of your senses will bring you closer to your dream. At the same time, it will be incredibly wonderful to bring with you a fantastic, "secret" image that you have created yourself, all about your dream, and your future.

Fantasy images can affect us just as much as the reality. So hold on to your fantasy image. And to make your image even more powerful and effective, why don't you add to it a serving of feelings? Look for the feelings that arise while you are "in" your image. What is it that brings forward your happiness? What is that gives you a feeling of harmony? What is it that makes your face crack into a huge smile? What is it that makes you bubble over with energy and gives you a good and dear feeling of well-being?

The reason why visualization is so powerful is that you create images in your consciousness where you see yourself together with and as a part of what you are dreaming of. You make thoughts and feelings just like they are real, just like as if you have had them.

The Incredible Power of Thoughts

All that we are is a result of what we have thought.

—*Buddha*

To understand the structure of the law, or better yet to make use of the law, it is important to see the system in how the law kicks in and becomes effective. As you now know, the law consists of three steps and all of the steps have their origin from your mind, just like everything else that happens and comes your way.

> **THE THREE STEPS ARE:**
> 1. Make your wish
> 2. Increase the frequencies—believe it is possible
> 3. Allow it to happen

"Thoughts are more powerful than a strong hand," says Sophocles. And for The Law of Possibilities to become effective for you, your thoughts are your important supporters and crucial for the outcome. Thoughts come, thoughts go, thoughts enlarge, thoughts disappear, thoughts are secret, thoughts are communicated, and thoughts do something to you. The thoughts are yours. If you wish to change your circumstances, you have to change your thoughts first.

Have you ever thought of something that didn't particularly please you and the more you thought about it, the worse it got? It is because The Law of Possibilities gives you more of the same thoughts, even when you have thought a negative thought.

If you, for a few moments, have been in touch with several equal thoughts and they all have been negative, then the situation will seem like it is even worse than it really is. And the more you think of it, the more upset you get.

It is just the same way with the good and positive thoughts. You have surely been in love at one time or another and I am pretty sure you will agree with me that there is almost no better situation to be in. Intoxicated with infatuation, you find yourself to be in a fantastically wonderful flow of positive, active thoughts and the more you think of the one you are in love with, the more positive thoughts come your way. You find your sweetheart to be the most wonderful thing that has ever happened to you, everything about him, or her, is simply fantastic. He's got such beautiful eyes, lovely skin, he's so incredibly kind and warm—there are really no limits to how fantastic your sweetheart is. In this situation too, you attract more of the thoughts you nurture; equal attracts equal. You are in a flow of positive thoughts, and you also get more of them. The same thing can happen if you are in a relationship where you find your partner to be unsexy and hopeless. Here, just like in the opposite situation, it will be of great importance for your well-being to find what it is with the other person that you really appreciate. You have to change your focus to what it is that you do find wonderful, and you will come to the realization that your environment changes in line with your own changes. Again you always get more of what you radiate. So what is it that you do want more of? Always go within yourself before you criticize others. That's when you will change, keep, or maintain your own, good energy, and that's actually what it's all about.

The quantum particles are in touch, the connection is there, and they are being reciprocated. You become what you think and what you think about the most you also attract. The life you are living right now is a reflection of the thoughts you have thought earlier. The positive thoughts and all those thoughts that weren't as good for you. That's why, by looking at your life as it is right now, you will find the answers to what has been your most dominant thoughts.

If you, for some reason or another, are in a situation you aren't satisfied with, you can at this very instant start to adopt The Law of Possibilities. To learn a more advantageous and helpful way of living, you can with your newly acquired knowledge of The Law of Possibilities change everything. But you have to make a decision to use the power of positive thinking. I will urge you to decide on something positive soon, because thoughts become reality!

In the same way as sound waves, your thoughts are waves too. If you compare yourself to a radio tower, it will be with the same frequency as you emit your thoughts, in which they will be answered with. What you emit, you get back. If you wish to change something in your life, it is recommended to switch the channel and change the frequency you use to send out your thoughts.

View The Law of Possibilities as a law of nature that doesn't separate the good thoughts from the bad. Look at the law as something that receives your thoughts and returns to you more of the thoughts you are thinking. As I have mentioned before, the law does not distinguish thoughts like "don't do," "don't," or "no." The law, however, provides you with more of what you are thinking. Maybe you even have been in a situation in which you have thought just like this; I will gladly speak for myself. With a smile, I will admit to being in situations where my thoughts have not always been the most appropriate. There was, for instance, no coincidence that I spilled tomato sauce on my white shirt yesterday. Just seconds before I did it, I had visited the thought that I should be careful not to spill, because it would be such a hard stain to remove. You might even recognize yourself, as you read some of the examples that will follow. Because in the same way you think negative thoughts, it is what the law receives from you it will give you more of. It will be useful to practice something else than just being good at sports.

"I can't be late."
(Becomes: I will be late.)

"Now, I have to be mindful so that I don't spill on the new tie."
(Becomes: I will spill on the new tie.)

"Don't do that to me."
(Becomes: Do that to me.)

"I have to be careful so that I don't catch a cold."
(Becomes: I have to catch a cold.)

"Vacation at last—I hope I don't get sick."
(Becomes: Vacation at last—I will get sick.)

"I don't want to argue anymore."
(Becomes: I want to argue more.)

"In my exam, I will surely be quizzed on a subject I don't know that well"
(Becomes: I want to be quizzed on a subject I don't know.)

"There certainly won't be any parking spaces along Main Street."
(Becomes: I don't want a parking space along Main Street, I would rather have to walk far.)

"That golf course is so incredibly difficult."
(Becomes: I will play lousy on that course.)

"It is for certain that I will not get the job I applied for."
(Becomes: I will not get that job, someone else will.)

> The Law of Possibilities will give you more of what you are thinking of, so I will repeat: What is it you want?
>
> The Law of Possibilities will simply give you what you focus on.

With this fabulous knowledge, you can actually change every little occurrence in your life. So what are you waiting for? Make up your mind to start your own little training camp to achieve better and more enjoyable weekdays. Practice leads you toward what it is you really are dreaming of. Everything is just a short or a long practice round away. And if you want it enough, you can do it. Just like my dearly beloved husband so beautifully put it when his job vanished from underneath his feet a few years ago: "I really had to be shook up from my roots to start with what I really have been dreaming of working with for years." Could it be expressed more clearly? The new possibilities were there, but disguised as huge challenges.

Practice what really matters in life. Practice being what you really want to be and don't wait until you completely stumble and fall before you start taking new measures. There are different situations or experiences that trigger people to act and many times I have wondered why so many people have to be set so far back before they do make changes in their lives. Sometimes extremes such as illness, being burned out, being laid off, or corresponding situations have to take place before they take charge of their own situation. It is you and only you that can help yourself in challenging situations. You might very well get input from other helpers, but in the end it is you that have to work yourself past the challenge. So what is it that you need to do to take a hold of yourself before your challenges becomes too much for you?

In my work as a coach, I have discovered that what most people find themselves stuck in is their own thoughts, thoughts on what they can't do, thoughts on what they wish was different, thoughts on what is challenging, thoughts that have repeated to themselves and over the years have become patterns—and for many, very inappropriate patterns.

Still, the most characteristic common feature is that many people are stuck in their inner dialogue, the conversations they are having with themselves, that often goes like this: "I have tried so many times before, but I cannot do it. I wish things were different, I'm not good enough, everyone else is so much better than me. That assignment is too big, I'm not sure if I can do it. I'm too fat. I've got too many wrinkles. Now that I am 50, it's all downhill. Everything is so hard." This is how they go on, infecting themselves deeper and deeper with worry-viruses. They nourish the negative frequencies and just get more of them. That's why it is so important that you take measures before more negative frequencies come your way. Everything you nurture, you get more of. If you do think that from now on it's all downhill, then that's what it is going to be like. You have chosen the thought and the thoughts will materialize themselves by giving you more of what you're thinking. Maybe you look at yourself in the mirror every morning and say "yuck" before you go to work, instead of seeing your beautiful face, throwing your arms out in the air, and telling yourself how great you really are. So a little, or a lot, if that's how you see it, is all it takes to have an impact on how your day will be.

Everything that happens to you starts with a thought, and thoughts will come flying through the air toward you in all kinds of strange situations. Do they really come flying, or is it you that choose to invite them in? Thoughts are really just words that are put together and that are traveling along the roads of your inner landscape. This is, at least, where the words that come out of your mouth comes from, which make you able to communicate with the rest of the world around you. Some will also actively use finger- or body language as well, but most of all your communication will reveal a lot about your inner landscape.

We relate to thoughts that become words in the form of frequencies which in turn arouse feelings.

Picture yourself squeezing a lemon. Before you even have tasted the juice that comes out of the lemon, you know that it will be sour because you already have had that experience. You can even "sense" the sourness so much that it makes your mouth water. You might relate to other incidents in life in just the same way. A thought is thought, familiar or unfamiliar, you receive an experience and the feeling for the experience makes itself known fairly quickly. Sometimes even quicker than you would like it to. It all ends at best with an action. I want to remind you that we humans have an average of 60,000 automatic reactions throughout the course of a day. Now that we know that our actions are a consequence of our language, it could be quite useful to have a closer look at how we speak with and to ourselves. So how do you speak with yourself?

To be able to fully live in accordance with the law, it will be worthwhile to be attentive of your thoughts and your reactions to what happens to you in life. Is it an inappropriate or an appropriate behavior that brings you your experiences? What do you focus on? What do you nurture? What do you want to change? What do you want to keep as it is? My recommendation is to become more playful and curious. If you apply The Law of Possibilities, you will also open up to taking an active part of life "now," instead of sitting stuck in yesterday or expecting something about the future.

Equal attracts equal.

What you radiate, you get more of.

A lot of people find it easier to order products from a catalogue or off the Internet than to decide what they want out of life. The most important area for many people is to become happy in life, to strut with happiness and excess energy, and to know what they will be when they "grow up." There are just as many adults as kids in this category and that's how it continues. A lot of them can't find this happiness, simply because they don't express it clearly or distinctively enough. So what are you really saying when you say the word happiness? What is it that you are thinking when you want more happiness? What is it that you really want? What is happiness for you? What is it that really makes you happy?

What is it that you are good at that you also enjoy doing? This is another big and important question you need to ask yourself.

> *Nothing in life is worth doing if you don't have fun doing it.*
> *—John Paul DeJoria*

It is important to be clear and precise, and to be versatile. Soon there will be examples for you from real life situations, experienced by people every day, people walking around with you somewhere out there in the world, so that you too will want to go out and make your own experiences, to take your first steps on the road to better days and a more positive life.

Take your valuable steps in your new direction and start working on the new edition of yourself. I send you wishes of a big serving of faith and lots of decisiveness, when others around you do not think that the law is effective.

I can surely guarantee that you will meet people that don't believe in the law, so already at this point, you should decide on how you will react to negative input.

For you to be able to stay in touch with your belief, you also need power. You have to have faith in that the law will work for you too, not just for others. That's when you can test the law, because you believe it is possible. If you're there, you've made a huge step forward in the right direction. That's when you make the important decisions yourself and turn what you are reading over into actions. It is not until it is put into action that new knowledge comes into its own. Action that is challenging in itself will, in many instances, make new ideas and input them in your brain, ending up as valuable thoughts about what you learned or read. I'll challenge you: what is it you need, where you are now, that can make you act according to the law?

Do Your Own "Spring-cleaning"

In the process of getting The Law of Possibilities to work for you, it could be worthwhile for you to clean up "your house." Put in a different way, you will have great joy from having a major "spring-cleaning" of your "hard drive." So that you can have more room for new and more appropriate thoughts. To start off a new beginning, it can be effective to clean up and throw away old thoughts. Make sure you go through your thoughts to decide which thoughts are advantageous and you need to preserve—which thoughts you need to polish and shine so that they can sparkle more and which thoughts that you will be happy to get rid of and throw away for good. You simply do not need to carry all of your thoughts with you at all times.

It has taken me a few years to realize that we have come to life to enjoy it: to learn, grow, and develop our soul. And being challenged with new thoughts and new knowledge is the same as growing and getting new possibilities.

It is with thoughts as it is with things you buy. If you buy new things all of the time, but never throw out the old things, then pretty quickly your closets and drawers will be filled to the brim. The same thing will happen to your head as you store more and more knowledge without turning it into practical action. If you store more and more knowledge, like many of us do, then the left half of your brain will grow bigger and bigger while there is plenty of room for innovation in the right half of your brain. It speaks for itself—when the distribution in between the brain halves becomes lopsided, then the interaction in between them will suffer also, and you do not function in the way you could have done. Everything in life can, with advantage, be used for learning and personal development. Together, logic and creativity will help you achieve more balance and harmony, fewer worries, and more happiness.

Ten Inspiring Possibilities

The parking possibility	The sweetheart possibility
The examination possibility	The bring-order-to-your-life possibility
The working-abroad possibility	The focus possibility
The career possibility	The change possibility
The health possibility	The entrepreneur possibility

It is inspiring to hear other people's stories about success and change. It will strengthen your own motivation, security, and faith in that something works. So what will be more natural for you, to be in the phase you are in now, or to participate in other people's life journeys together with the law?

Fantasies and dreams are everything.
They are images of the coming highlights of life.
—*Albert Einstein*

I choose to start off with a few of my own parking stories because they are true and at the same time it is something that you too can do, to go out in the world and obtain your own similar personal experiences. All you need is a driver's license so that you can drive a car. The next thing you need is a parking space for the car you are driving, some place, somewhere that only you know of.

If you don't have access to a car, you can change the example and dream that someone will offer you a cup of coffee or an ice cream—send out your frequencies and see what happens.

The Parking Possibility

The dream:

I Ask for a Parking Space for My Car at Exactly the Place Where I am Going to

Start with something small so that you do get your first experiences with the law. Then you can increase your wishes as your confidence that the law works expands within you. The parking space can be just the way to get started. To make your wish come true, you just simply need to know where it is you dream of getting a parking space for your car. It might be the day that you are going downtown to an important meeting in the city you live in. Now it is so that the meeting will take place in an office in one of the busiest streets of the city. There are parking meters nearby, but there are not a lot of them and today you want to find a spot right outside the building you are going to.

The first step of the law usually begins at home or at the office or wherever it is you are and preferably before you get into the car to head toward your destination. You apply the law by focusing and bringing your attention to your need for a parking space close by your destination or right outside the front door. It is important that you are very clear and distinct. The best option will be to decide whether the spot should be right in front or close by. That's how clear you have to dare to be.

The next step of the law is to increase the frequencies, so let us make use of your sense of vision and visualize. Now you see before you, and preferably as an image, the parking space you want. You see the entrance of your destination, you see the parking meters, and you see before your inner eye that one of these parking spaces is available for you. If you don't know the surroundings of where you are going, you can still use the same technique. You continue by increasing the frequencies and telling yourself that it is going to work out. The feelings fall in place and you are where you need to be.

In the end, you are to feel that you have full confidence in that you will find an available space for your car, which is the third step of the law. You simply trust that there will be a spot for you in the image that you have processed in advance. Get in the car and drive happily off toward the meeting in full confidence that there is an available space for you once you get there. When you arrive, don't be surprised and amazed that there actually is an available space for you, or that a car that has been parked is just about to pull out of its spot and make it available for you. It just might happen that there isn't an available spot the very second you arrive. Then just circle around the block and be observant.

What does it mean to be observant in this situation? Be observant to the motions in the picture: there's a person with keys in his hand, or that guy over there is headed toward one of the parked cars, or there's a car with an open door, or over there, there are two people right next to a car talking to each other. So be aware of what is going on in the "picture."

You will start to experience your friends exclaiming: "Oh, that's just typically you; you always get a spot for your car right out front." Or: "I can't believe it; you always almost drive straight through the door."

What kind of virus is it that you are reading about now? I will happily share with you that this is a parking possibility from my own life, and that I myself always use The Law of Possibilities no matter where it is I am about to park my car. Even in a parking garage or a parking lot, I will radiate the confidence in that I quickly will find a spot.

While working with this book, I heard of the parking story of some people I know very well that wanted to try the law for the very first time. They were two young couples going to a movie theater in the middle of downtown. In the area surrounding the movie theater, there was a lot of construction and several of the parking spaces were temporarily removed. In the middle of downtown, headed for the movies, they decided to give the "Anne-Mette" method, as they called it, a try. They all looked at each other with a little smile across their face and decided that they wanted a spot for their car right outside the theater. They all nurtured their thoughts with positive frequencies and full confidence, and they agreed that all the four of them should do it. And guess what? When the car was parked right in front of the movie theater, they all ascertained that the law works.

I have another wonderful parking story from my dearest oldest son. He'd just turned 18 and was standing there with a steaming fresh driver's license in his hand. At that time, he was attending a school in the middle of the city and what was more natural than him wanting to drive to school. A very concrete and distinct wish that he did have fulfilled too. Proud as a peacock, he jumped into the car.

It was one of his first trips into the city by himself, and he felt like a king. On the road, while headed to school in the morning traffic, the thoughts of a parking space entered his mind. He was to park in a part of the city where it is notoriously difficult to find parking, no matter what hour of day it is and he started wondering where on earth he was going to park and additionally, getting to school on time. Some challenge. Sitting in the traffic jam, he thought: I'll call my mom. "Got any ideas of where to park, mom?" In my world, there exists something called The Law of Possibilities, so I said: "Would you consider taking part in a little experiment, today?" Sure, yeah, he could do that. Where you are right now, think that there is an available parking space right outside school, visualize, create an image of the parking space you want, I explained. "Ok, I'm willing to give it a shot," he replied. At 9:02, my cell phone beeped with a text message: "I parked the car right outside school, and I made it to my first class :-)." Lovely, I thought, and as soon as he got home I asked him: "Do you believe a little bit more in The Law of Possibilities now, my son, now that you have experienced that it works?" "Um, ah, well yes, kinda sort of ... but I am not sure if it was that law that helped me."

A very human reaction, when trying out the law for the first time, but maybe it is all about trying it over and over again to have the fantastic qualities of the law confirmed. I am sure that you will agree with me on the fact that no elite athlete or successful businesswoman will climb right to the top at their very first attempt. There has to be a dream, a lot of faith, a positive attitude, trust, and practice to do it. That's the way it is with The Law of Possibilities too.

> **THE PARKING POSSIBILITY IS FOR THOSE WHO**
> - want to have their first experiences with The Law of Possibilities,
> - wonder how to get started,
> - want a practical day-to-day life,
> - always find themselves short on time,
> - think it will be exciting to explore The Law of Possibilities,
> - don't want parking tickets,
> - have a big helping of curiosity of themselves, and life,
> - want to walk the shortest distance possible,
> - want to discover something magical.

What you can achieve:

You will always find room for your car, wherever you decide it should be.

The challenges you might face:

Do you believe it is possible, or do you call it nonsense?

What you specifically can do:

Create a visual image before you start your journey.

Nourish the image by thinking positive thoughts about it.

Have confidence.

Play with the possibilities as you go, in the queue or anywhere.

Don't be surprised if it really happens.

When:

Right now, or anytime you will have a need for a parking space.

Let us move on and have a look at some other areas in life in which The Law of Possibilities has been put to good use.

This is the story of Daniel. One year, I was fortunate to have been his mentor. Daniel was in his last year of studying in a bachelor degree course in Finances. He's a hardworking student with ambitious goals. He's the student that puts in the work to achieve A's and B's in his subjects. But in the examination possibility you now will be taking part in, his goal was completely different. His dream was to pass the exam. And as you as an observant reader already have discovered, The Law of Possibilities can be used regardless of whether the level of your wishes are high or low, the most important is what you want. And Daniel knew what he wanted; he wanted to pass his exam. It's not always about being the first, the best, or reaching the furthest, but about deciding what it is you want to accomplish. The law works regardless.

The Examination Possibility

The dream:

I Want to Pass My Examination

In connection with his oral examination in the subject "Financial changes and applied macroeconomics," Daniel will have use for The Law of Possibilities again. Together we had worked with how he should make use of The

Law of Possibilities for his exam around Christmas time, but then in a completely different framework than now. Earlier he had worked more on visualizing the day of his exam—to picture himself and visualize the room, to see himself as happy, smiling, and content with the assignment, to see before himself writing his paper with the ink literally spluttering out of the pen—another sign of him being pleased with the assignment. He had seen himself in the image called "the examination day" for in that way to connect with himself and to be at his best when it really counts.

The time just after Christmas, at where he was now, with his final exam just around the corner—and not the final exam for just this term, but the final exam of three years of studies—everything turned out a little bit different than he had planned. Daniel had made a plan for the examination period that involved spending two weeks in preparation. What he had not planned was that his fiancée would find herself face to face with her great opportunity in life. In addition to her final music and drama studies in London, she had also entered an audition. The winner would get nothing less but to perform the leading role in a big musical appearing on The National Theatre. His fiancée did so well that she, right in the middle of Daniel's exam period, faced the possibility of being among those who got through the eye of the needle and would get the chance to participate in the final rounds broadcast on TV later that autumn. It would be the final and crucial round to choose the female leading role. This opportunity could also be seen as an investment in future job possibilities in a field where jobs don't exactly grow on trees. For Daniel, the time to do his exam preparations shrunk from two weeks to two days, because it became very important for him to support his fiancée and to be there for her during her "exam." A simple choice but also a challenging decision to make with regard to his own examinations.

Daniel knew parts of the curriculum very well, but he also knew that he did not know the subject financial changes as well as he should. He had read 2 out of 11 chapters and parts of 3 out of 10 articles, but as he said himself, "I had a feeling that I would make it, even though I normally would have panicked." Daniel's thoughts were guided toward the three parts of the curriculum that he had studied and at the same time he sent out the dream of being examined in the parts of the curriculum he knew he was familiar with.

This being an oral exam, he met two of his fellow students as agreed half an hour early on the examination day to go through a simulation model with them that he did not fully understand. One of his co-students pointed out that there was stagflation in the last period of that model. For you as a reader, it is not important that you comprehend what this is all about, but it is essential to the story. Daniel himself could not grasp it completely either, but never the less, it turned out to become a very vital piece of information for him anyway. The first question he was asked during his examination, from one of his three censors, was exactly a question in which the correct reply was: stagflation. This answer leads the censor to hand the floor over to the next censor after just one question. Daniel mastered the challenges of the second censor fairly well. The last of the three censors was to question him on the subject of financial changes, and as we know, this is where Daniel was the least prepared. However, there was one part of the subject financial changes that he did know well, which is the bank crisis of the 1920s. He had made use of The Law of Possibilities to increase the probability of being questioned on exactly this part of the curriculum. The Law of Possibilities proved itself to work for him again, because events did turn out in such a way that he actually was tested on the bank crisis of the 1920s. That's when he understood that he would be able to "pull ashore" the exam. It goes along with this story that there is no other grade that he has ever been more delighted to receive than the grade he got on his exam. He got a C, which definitely is more than barely passing. His teachers knew that Daniel normally wouldn't be satisfied with this grade, so Daniel kept his happiness within himself as he headed out the door of the classroom, but as soon as the door closed behind him he let all of his cheerfulness out. As he expressed it himself: "An outrageously delightful experience."

To release and let loose all of the joy you feel is the same as celebrating and saying thank you—something that is very important to get The Law of Possibilities over on your side for good.

Daniel also has a little additional story to share about staying in touch with friends, and the well-known phrase: "it's so funny that I heard from you right now, because I was just thinking of you today." Now you know that this phrase is all about the energy you radiate, which is responded to because you once have established an energy connection that still exists, with the person at the other end. This story is about Facebook, the Internet craze spreading itself across the country like wildfire, a social utility that allows you to "connect" with friends virtually on the Internet by creating your own profile. The system is closed in such a manner that you have to allow your friends to link up with you and vice versa. This story is about wishing to get back in touch with five friends that he had neither seen nor heard from since high school. On the actual day, he starts out by sending out lots of thoughts to the friends he has in mind, thinking about how nice it would be to have them linked to his profile on the Internet. What's funny is that during the next few days, already the first week, one of the old friends he has in mind beats him to it and invites him to become a friend on his profile. Their friendship was restored, old relations became as new, and the other four friends joined in shortly after too.

As Daniel said it, without having his mind on the law as he speaks: "I can't really believe it, here I go sending them some thoughts, and then all of this suddenly happens." Or maybe it is the law working?

I have no doubts about it, the law states clearly that equal attracts equal, even in these situations and circumstances.

THE EXAMINATION POSSIBILITY IS FOR THOSE WHO
- want to achieve the grades they really want,
- want to improve their existing grades,
- want to read with attentiveness,
- have not studied their entire curriculum,
- know what they want to do when they "grow up,"
- want to attend the school they are dreaming of,
- want to practice awareness and focus,
- want to explore new ways of thinking,
- want to have time for their sweetheart too.

What you can achieve:

Use the law when you wish to be examined on a specific topic or when you are in a situation where you only know parts of the curriculum that you will be tested on. You can certainly use it if you know your entire subject really well too and it doesn't matter too much to you either.

The challenges you might face:

Yourself and your faith in the law that it really works.

What you specifically can do:

Decide which parts of the curriculum you would prefer or want to be questioned on.

When:

Your next exam, the next one after that, or even the one after that again or ... on and on and on.

Your objection now might sound like this: sure, but what happens if everybody makes use of the law with regard to the same exam, that won't work? Then you should know that the person with the strongest wishes and dreams will have their dream fulfilled.

According to my experience, young people are more open to the fact that the law works, rather than what older generations are. The young ones hear about the law, they are fearless, they try it out, and they get quick results. They quickly discover joy and happiness. The reason to this might be that young people aren't in touch with a lot of the objections and the automatic thoughts that so many adults carry around with them. The doubts and the skepticism that many adults have within themselves, or that the principles of "just who do you really think you are?" (The Law of Jante) has embossed into the adult generation, is something that a lot of young people are happily free from. Young people are more curious and fearless, they try things out, they learn, and they move on. You can have it just like this even if you are an adult too, but you might have to figure out what it is that's blocking you from opening up to new learning about life, to prevent it from becoming new learning that's just stored in your left brain half as new knowledge.

I recommend that you replace The Law of Jante with The Anti-law of Jante, and it goes like this:

THE ANTI-LAW OF JANTE

- Remember that you are special and unique.
- Remember that no one can measure what you are worth.
- Remember that you have the knowledge.
- Remember that you have insights and experiences that nobody else has.
- Remember that there is a lot of things that you have every reason to be proud of.
- Remember that you can.
- Remember that you have the ability to tolerate others.
- Remember that there are many people that like you.
- Remember that you know and can do something that you can teach others.
- Accept yourself and accept others!

Dare to be a little bit more playful and youthful, and open up to allowing yourself more space in your own life.

The Working-abroad Possibility

The dream:

I Want to Work in Another Country

The story of Runa starts with one of my earlier coaching clients recommending me to one of her friends. She feels it would benefit her friend to have someone outside of her circle of friends and family to help her make some important life choices. Runa, the lady in this story, contacted me one winter's day to ask for help to achieve her dream of working abroad again. She needed help breaking out of the familiar and safe routine, as she calls it.

Runa had for many years felt restless and had been in touch with feelings of having something undone or unfinished. But to dare to go as far as to realize the dream was such a big step that she eventually felt that she needed help. As you will learn from this story, you do not always have to do everything on your own.

Early on in our coaching relationship, I introduced Runa to The Law of Possibilities because in life there were several areas that Runa would benefit from getting better acquainted with herself and how she was thinking about what happens to her in life. The first thing I heard was a person that would have a great advantage of starting to have a more positive conversation with herself, a conversation that could praise her for all the things she was able to achieve, that more often would tell her she was beautiful, that she would be able to be more playful, that happiness was to be found everywhere if she would only look for it, and that the job in a foreign country would be right around the corner. At first, it became important to have a look at what Runa didn't want more of: her worry-viruses. By working herself through her worry-viruses, she came up with a list consisting of many items that augmented what it is she really wanted and at the top of this list was her dream of working abroad again.

In the middle of this process, while she was making a list of her dreams and gradually starting to allow more of what she wants in life, she receives a tip about an exciting job opportunity within the German travel industry. After a while, she became well acquainted with the law, and her awareness showed great progress. She had even made herself a book where she had made notes of her possibility-viruses so that she could remind herself of The Law of Possibilities' way of thinking and its mind-set whenever she needed it. She learned how important it was to practice and to allow the process. Because if there was one thing she wanted very dearly, it was to let more contentment into her life, which, for her, was a very important element in her journey toward a good and secured life.

Today she has a very exciting job in Hamburg, Germany, and she says that The Law of Possibilities has become a very important part of her life. The law has taught her a new way of thinking that she really values and appreciates. Positive thinking has become a valuable way of life that she is using toward her next dream which is to find her dream apartment in her new city.

She has pictured the details of what the apartment should look like, where it is to be situated, close to a lake, the number of rooms, what the kitchen looks like and in this way, she has gone further by making use of the law. As I am writing these words, I do not know exactly how the process is moving along, but I do know that she has sent out her wishes and is nurturing them with faith. Now she knows that things will fall into place when the time is right. Simultaneously she is living a better life with positive thinking and a conviction of herself as a valuable human being.

> **THE WORKING-ABROAD POSSIBILITY CAN BE USED BY THOSE WHO**
> - are dreaming of another job,
> - want to have a look at the job they have today with a new set of eyes,
> - want to do a little bit of daydreaming,
> - want to make some changes,
> - want to have more fun in their lives,
> - want to smile more often,
> - want something to strive for,
> - want a better life,
> - want to challenge themselves.

What you can achieve:

Use the law when you do have a dream job that you have not yet attained, or when you want to think new thoughts regarding your existing line of work.

The challenges you might face:

That you really do not know what your dream job is, or that you are stuck in the logic around your existing job situation but that your heart tells you differently.

What you specifically can do:

Describe the job that you are dreaming of, write it down, and believe that it is possible.

When:

Start today by making your mind up about something, or just smile and be happy and content with the job you've got.

Now that you have gotten some insight into how The Law of Possibilities can be utilized to get your dream job, the time has come to dream on. Let's have a look at another possibility that is all about reaching a new career within your existing profession.

The Career Possibility

The dream:

I Want a New Career and at the Same Time I Want to be Able to Continue to Make Use of My Education

On an autumn day in 2003, dentist Kristin has something that resembles a strong allergic reaction. It starts with a headache and tingling in the palm of her hands, and she starts to tremble violently. Her blood sugar oscillates and soon she cannot even stand up on her own two feet. She is put on a sick leave without anyone being able to tell what there is that's wrong with her. A few days earlier, Kristin had accidentally tested a so-called bioresonance machine, which registers if there are imbalances in your body while simultaneously it stimulates your body to heal itself.

The conclusion was that something was draining Kristin of her strength. She lacked a number of vitamins, minerals, and fatty acids, and there were several food items that she was intolerant of, including wheat flour. Kristin is quite sure that it was the machine that made her sick and completely unable to continue working as a dentist. Not for a second did she connect her problems with her work as a dentist or the fact that three–four years earlier had all of her amalgam fillings replaced because they were old and cracked.

She was out of work as a dentist for an entire year. She took vitamins and minerals, and changed her diet completely and thought about what she was going to do now that she couldn't work as a dentist anymore because her hands were still trembling.

During this time, she had a chat with one of her good friends and started dreaming of a new career. Where she was now in life, she wanted to focus on her future and her career. Kristin went at it with pencil and paper in hand and began to make a list of what a future career needed to consist of and include. There were a couple of things that clearly presented themselves. One thing was that she wanted to help other people and the second one was that she wanted to continue employing her dental knowledge and proficiency. These were two clearly defined possibility-viruses. But Kristin was still in a situation in which she could not use her hands in the same way as she used to. It was at some point in this phase that she, through acquaintances, got in touch with The United Nations Children's Fund (UNICEF: the world's largest charity for children's rights) and UNICEF is all about helping other people. Kristin slowly started to work for UNICEF, but she still felt that something just didn't feel quite right. Yes, it was about helping people, but for her part there was something missing and she sort of felt that it did not match up completely in the way it should for her. One thing was positive though: she was slowly but surely about to return, but it would still take some time before she got her redemption.

In the meantime, a friend of her visited and brought with her a book for her. It was about health and everything the pharmaceutical industry did not want published.

The book aroused Kristin's interest, and she started to connect her problems with the removal and replacement of her amalgam fillings a few years before. No one denies that mercury, one of the ingredients of amalgam, is poisonous. The Norwegian Pollution Control Authority and the Norwegian Minister of Environment (this story took place in Norway) had both suggested a ban against the use of amalgam fillings, which is included in a general proposal to prohibit the use of mercury in products. An increasing number of research reports suggest possible connections between mercury poisoning and feeling indisposed and weak, dizziness, headaches, and impaired short-time memory. All the experts do not agree on the issue, but to Kristin this made sense and her interest in the problem increased, especially with regard to her own health problems. What she now acquired as new knowledge within this field also made her start to attract other exciting people with skills in this particular area, one after another and in this way a new career "carpet" started to unfold itself out in front of her. Kristin's positive frequencies about her future career started to give her a possibility to use her competence, but now in a new way. In addition she could help other people with their health problems, something that she had always wanted to do. The Law of Possibilities gave her more of what it is she wanted. It is also part of the story that now there is a total ban against the use of amalgam in tooth fillings in Norway.

Kristin is now called a "transformed" dentist. She's back to work full time, and dentistry has taken on a new meaning for her. Now she thinks holistic, the mouth is after all just a part of our entire body. She helps people to have a better life. "I asked for the opportunity to help people to get better. Now I do it as a dentist again, but without the use of amalgam and for better health," Kristin says.

USE THE CAREER POSSIBILITY WHEN YOU

- know what you are dreaming of,
- want to do good deeds,
- have a set of skills you want to make more use of,
- know something that can be beneficial to others,
- want to develop within your area of expertise,
- want to use your skills out there in the world,
- want changes, but also want to continue to employ your competence,
- know how good you are and want more people to discover it,
- want to smile more often,
- know what you are dreaming of, but haven't achieved it yet.

What you can achieve:

Use the law when you discover that you are acquiring new knowledge and experiences that give you the possibility to grow professionally and you want to employ these new skills.

The challenges you might face:

That you might think that you are too old for innovation, or that you are stuck in the fact that what you know is the only accepted way of thinking in your professional field, or that you need scientific proof to change your system of belief.

What you specifically can do:

Allow yourself a deeper sense of curiosity, even though you know your field or profession very well. You can always look for positive development—not only academically, but personally also so that you grow as a human being.

When:

Is there really any need to wait? It is always important and valuable to be more curious and playful, and the road ahead of you is always filled with possibilities.

Just like Kristin's story tells us both about her new career and her recaptured health, you too can also work toward better everyday health, or simply just take even better care of your good health.

In January 2008, I held a two-hour lecture about The Law of Possibilities. About 40 people attended it. The audience was very interested and engaged, but the reactions that came after the lecture was finished meant even more to me. There's always someone from the audience that approaches me when I am done, but to have somebody running up toward you, throwing themselves around your neck, and telling you that you've changed their life in those two hours is a little bit more than I am used to. This person had a reaction that very much resembled my own when I was introduced to the law for the very first time. In a way, it was the words of the law and that it actually existed that was the last missing piece, the last key to the understanding of how everything in life is connected. She left with a happy soul, and I had done a good deed. Someone else too, a handsome, significant person of the business community came over to me and expressed her feelings with the words: "You just have to let me give you a hug, I am so grateful, and this was so amazing. What an exciting law! I want to use this law so much more."

There were several people that had an "aha" moment that day, and they all got some very worthwhile replenishment. I was very grateful myself too because I got to, as I like to think of it, sprinkle some valuable seeds out into the world—amongst the audience.

When people do get touched, something happens to them and it was in this way Birgit was sent my way by recommendation from someone in the audience.

Her story is fantastic and it says everything there is to know about the power of the mind and the importance of your subconscious when it comes to achieving your dreams, when you go along with them. This story might give all you doubters and skeptics a little reminder that there is more between heaven and earth than what we can explain with logic or pure science. There are many magical solutions to a lot of problems. In the same way, The Law of Possibilities can bring more magic and happiness into your life and maybe even challenge your rigid thoughts a little bit.

The Health Possibility

The dream:

I am Dreaming of a Full Recovery

Birgit worked as a homeopath when she became sick. She was diagnosed with hypothyroidism, declining function of the thyroid gland, which meant that her body went into slow motion. In addition, she got a big lump on her neck. The main symptoms were that she lost more or less all of her energy. Her body worked at reduced speed, she slept a lot, she easily gained weight, and she was told that she would have to expect to take hormone medicine for the rest of her life. This is an iodine containing medicine that's supposed to help her metabolism to do its job. She explained, among other things, like going to social functions in the evenings were a nightmare because she didn't have the strength to do it.

Her story shows us that our body is indeed a fantastically self-regulating system that wants to be on your side.

Just after Birgit got sick, she started to read books. She wanted to find out as much as she could about her disease and to understand how it all fits together. She devoured absolutely everything she could get her hands on that could be associated with the difficult situation she was in. As a homeopath, she had a connection to thinking outside of the box that there could be alternative methods and ways of thinking. So she tried healing, acupuncture, and acupressure, but without any effect. She studied how the brain works. No stone was to be left unturned, something that's not an unusual reaction when facing difficult life situations. She read about nutrition and got in touch with something called "dream board" about halfway into the course of her disease, without going deeper into it.

After six years, Birgit does something that will become the right "medicine" to recover again. She turns back to what she had read about dream boarding. This is like a "blackboard of goals," a kind of visualization technique. She starts by cutting out a picture of the upper body of a woman, with a neck without a lump on it. Then she cuts away the woman's face and replaces it with a facial image of herself.

Now for the first time in quite a while, she sees a picture of herself in a healthy body. She decides to hang this picture on her bedroom door so that she will see it every day, several times a day too. The picture is to give her a conscious and a subconscious experience of being fully recovered. As she is putting it up, she's reflecting on the fact that this is literally the first time in over six years that she sees an image of herself as 100 percent healthy and fully recovered, and this experience is to increase itself over the next five months. Because after five months pass what she calls a sudden occurrence of feeling a whole lot better happens. That's when she decides to also reduce her amount of medications. Together with a newfound strength and faith in that she will recover fully, the lump on her neck gradually becomes smaller and smaller. As she says herself:

she did no other changes than to continue to associate with the picture on her bedroom door. Shortly thereafter, she no longer needs any medicine anymore, and the lump is as good as gone. Since then she has been healthy and it is almost too good to be true and incomprehensible to anyone around her. She says like most of us that since she heard about The Law of Possibilities that was the first time she got an understanding of how her own healing process had even been possible.

Make a wish, define your dream, increase the frequencies, believe it is possible, and have faith in that your dreams will come true and become reality.

USE THE HEALTH POSSIBILITY WHEN YOU

- want to cooperate with your body,
- want to contribute to your own healing process,
- want more energy in your daily life,
- want to experience more wellness,
- have discovered that everything starts with a thought,
- generally want to feel better with yourself,
- want to feel more alive,
- need to speak nicely to yourself,
- need to deal with minor problems,
- want to shine a little bit more,
- want to be yourself, completely and fully,
- want to take care of your health.

What you can achieve:

You can recover from anything that's bothering you, if you allow positive thinking which in return creates positive feelings.

The challenges you might face:

That your belief and faith in yourself is not strong enough and that your worries are standing in your way, or that you find it challenging to find your confidence and to trust yourself. Your confidence and your belief in yourself is lurking around and just waiting to be put to use. You just have to make the choice.

What you specifically can do:

Make your own dream board, or write down your dreams in the present tense.

When:

Now or at once because staying healthy is amazingly important.

There are no limits to which areas of life The Law of Possibilities can be applied to. You can even use the law to find your ideal life companion. The reason why so many cannot find their dream partner has a lot to do with being unclear and not distinct enough. They don't take the time to sit down with a pen and paper in their hands to make notes, point by point, what personal characteristics that are important to them to have in their partner.

The story of Kjersti is such a story. After a divorce, which is not a very pleasant process for the most of us, Kjersti makes her wish list for what would later be an encounter with the man of her dreams. She makes use of The Law of Possibilities as a tool to avoid the many mistakes a lot of us do when we want to find a new life companion, without being clear and concise in what we want. The words "life companion" says very little or nothing about that person's character. This is the reason why so many that have left partners they did not get along with, attract new partners with the same personal characteristics as their last one. The Law of Possibilities is nurtured with negative frequencies and simply gives you more of the same. So, be clear, concise, and positive in your wishes, just like Kjersti was, just like her story shows us.

The Law of Possibilities will work splendidly no matter what your age is—young or old, tall or short, overweight or slim, it does not matter. The Law of Possibilities is for everyone.

The Sweetheart Possibility

The dream:

Above Anything on Earth, I Wish to Find and to Have the Greatest Love of All Back into My Life Again

One evening, Kjersti and a friend of hers were discussing life in general, men and love in particular. Kjersti reaches the conclusion that she has always aimed high regarding her job and her career. She had always embraced the possibilities that had come her way, which had resulted in exciting and challenging work opportunities. However, on the subject of love she had had relatively low ambitions. She had sought security and she felt that she had sacrificed a lot for love, freshly divorced as she was now. During the conversation she had with her friend that evening, she thought that now would be the time to aim high in love, to find the greatest love of all. With one marriage behind her, she knew a great deal about what it is she wanted in a future partner.

Her friend gave her a piece of advice what would turn out to become very valuable. She encouraged Kjersti to write down just how she wanted the man of her dreams to be—completely in accordance with what The Law of Possibilities recommends for achieving success.

At the top of the sheet of paper she's writing on, she jots down: humor, laughter, the ability to make me laugh, and then her pen just starts running wild. For you to be able to see what a wish list like this could look like, Kjersti is generously sharing her wish list with you.

What Do I Want in a Man?

WORRY-VIRUSES	POSSIBILITY-VIRUSES
	• Humor—the ability to make me laugh, feel joy. • Wisdom—has thought a lot of things through and wants to share his thoughts with me. • Warmth, empathy, and care. • Position, success (I have to admit to this). • Good sex and desire. • A Man! • The look, the eyes—eye contact. • Magic—the feeling of "being meant to be." • Big, strong, and hair on his chest. • The ability to express love and confirming it regularly.

WORRY-VIRUSES	POSSIBILITY-VIRUSES
	• Tenderness and closeness. • Togetherness to enjoy each other's successes and unity. • Like to travel—see and learn. • Secure in himself so that he dares to/can give me freedom. • Common interests. • Like to do the same things, sporty. • Clean and well-dressed, but not pretentious and snobbish.

As you can see from this example, Kjersti went straight on to the possibility-viruses. She didn't consider it necessary to have to go through the worry-viruses and that's perfectly fine.

The list only consists of positive statements about the personal characteristics of the man of her dreams, completely in line with what you need to do to make The Law of Possibilities work for you in life.

When these two friends left each other that evening, Kjersti put her list in her purse and headed for home. The day after she took her list out again to have another look at what she had written the previous evening. She laughed a little bit to herself and actually felt a little embarrassed as she described it. That there really would be such a man seemed quite impossible. The thoughts flying through her head were that what was on that list seemed a little bit too incredible. And would she, Kjersti, ever have a chance on finding such a man—if he existed and would she ever meet him? She felt that the list might even be a bit silly with all of its details.

Kjersti still decided to have faith in her wish list and sent off her wishes into the universe. She put the actual list aside and didn't really think much more of it.

Just six months after the list was created, Kjersti met a fantastic and handsome man. They agreed to meet for a cup of coffee the day after they met. Over coffee, they got to become better acquainted. The conversation flowed easily and was very rewarding and Kjersti had thoughts that this is the man that she had been dreaming about.

A few weeks after their first date, Kjersti gets her list out again. She hasn't had a look at it since it was written half a year earlier and she's almost knocked off her feet. The list describes in detail the man she is so head over heels in love with. There's nothing on the list that doesn't match up with the man that she has just gotten to get better acquainted with. She says that there is a 100 percent correlation between the list and the man that she now shares her love with, the man she finds to be completely fantastic, and with whom she will happily share the rest of her life.

This man of her dreams has a few other characteristics that she values as well, that she hadn't put on the list. She had often thought that the new man in her life should also have an impulsive and spontaneous personality too, but nevertheless, she didn't put those qualities on her list. Whenever she, although very rarely, gets a little bit annoyed that the new man in her life does not have these traits as part of his personality, she has to remind herself that she hadn't put them on her wish list, either. In other words, she got exactly the man she "ordered." And then, what more could you ask for?

Kjersti was not familiar with The Law of Possibilities when she made her wish list. But in retrospect, she can see the connection and she has no doubts whatsoever that it is using The Law of Possibilities that the man of her dreams has been sent her way. For Kjersti, as well as it is for me and many others, everything becomes obvious as soon as we learn about The Law of Possibilities. Then there are so many things that receive a renewed sense and fall into place. To be familiar with the law makes it so much easier to actively make use of it and to make it into a conscious way of life.

There is nothing you cannot be, do, or get.

USE THE SWEETHEART POSSIBILITY WHEN YOU
- want to find your own dream man or woman,
- want to connect closer to the love you have for yourself,
- know that now, love can come your way too,
- have tried everything else and nothing else works,
- want to be on the lighter side of life,
- really want to have a partner,
- find it fitting,
- wish for a really good friend,
- wish for a hiking or walking companion,
- dream of sharing your life with someone,
- want a travel companionship,
- would like to have a pet,
- feel that you have love to share.

What you can achieve:

You can find your dream partner once you decide how you would like your sweetheart to be, or how you want the person to be for you to want to share your friendship and love with him or her.

The challenges you might face:

That you have a tendency to make things a lot harder than they actually are.

What you specifically can do:

Simply: pen, paper, and honesty to yourself.

When:

As soon as you feel ready for it.

I gave a lecture one day and it gave me so many exciting and wonderful encounters with people that had experiences with using The Law of Possibilities. My clients distributed invitations of my lecture to potential participants and in connection with this an invitation was sent to a friend of Johanne. This next story will be about her. Her friend saw that I would be holding a lecture about The Law of Possibilities, something that Johanne was very interested in as well. The conversation ended with me inviting her to join the lecture too. The result of us meeting each other turned into yet another exciting relation for the both of us and another fantastic story about how the use of The Law of Possibilities will bring incredible experiences to those who dare to step out of their comfort zone and who dare to push the boundaries of what they believe is possible in life.

The Bring-order-to-your-life Possibility

The dream:

I Dream of Finding the Best Way of Living My Life

This story is about Johanne and how she has made use of the law in areas such as living abroad and work—all to reach her dreams.

Johanne was born in Australia and grew up in Northern Ireland. Her education was in the field of applied chemistry, something that brought her to meet the greatest love of her life, who in turn brought her to Seattle in the United States. Johanne worked for a pharmaceutical company in Ireland when she met her great love, an American who worked in the same company as she did, but in the United States. They met each other in Dublin and fell head over heels in love with each other. The relationship was kept alive across the Atlantic Ocean for three months by phone and letters, when he returned to Ireland for another nine-month stay. During this time, they lived together and they decided to get married before he had to return to the United States again. The day they were to leave for the United States together, Johanne was stopped and held back at the airport because her paperwork was not in order. She was told that the application process for a green card may very well take up to six months. Her husband was able to postpone his departure for five days before he was to return to work in Seattle. The honeymoon turned into five days in Dublin and not in the United States as they both had wanted. Her husband then had to leave, while she remained in Ireland without knowing when she would be able to see him again.

Johanne took on The Law of Possibilities, unknowingly aware of its existence. She made use of it in exactly the way one should do to be able to achieve their dreams. She visualized, she created an image of seeing herself together with her husband in Seattle, in the United States. She spent a lot of energy picturing her reunion with him. Against all the odds, the most incredible thing happened; she got the go-ahead that she could leave after just five weeks. Hard to believe that six months had turned into just five weeks.

After seven years in the United States, Johanne is again faced with having to make new life choices. She and her husband have grown apart. They have had to realize and come to the conclusion that they were too different from each other and that in order to give each other peace they have to set each other free. Around the time their relationship ends, there are a lot of things that happen to Johanne that are not positive. Her car is stolen and she loses her job, all of which are signs that she thinks that something in her life needs to be changed. At the end of her marriage, she spent a lot of time making lists of how she wants her life to be in the future. With regard to work, she wants to use all of her talents. She was also willing to be shown a new path in life and to do all the changes she had to do to achieve it. She made lists of everything she was good at and she went on like this without having direct knowledge of the law. She was to learn of its existence at a later time. Surprisingly she was using the law in the way it is intended to be used.

Her energy begins to return. She learned that being in a relationship that does not work uses up a lot of your own energy. Now her energy is on its way back.

On a work visit to Budapest, she met someone who would become important to her. She was there for one week with work and stayed for an extra week to see more of Europe.

On her flight across the Atlantic Ocean, on her way to Budapest, she noticed a man sitting in the row in front of her on the plane. She hadn't even finished the thought of how she felt she would like to sit in the same row, when a lady pointed out to her that she was in the wrong seat and that she should be in the row ahead—right next to the man she'd seen a few moments earlier. The man turned out to be Dutch living in Norway. He invited her to pay him a visit the next time she is back in Europe.

A year later, Johanne decides to visit Oslo in Norway. The surrounding areas of Oslo has lots of mountains and lakes, forests with pine trees, and all of the people she met were friendly. She had arrived in a city surrounded by everything she had put on her wish list. She realized she wanted to live in Norway.

When back in the United States, she decides that it is in Norway that she wants to settle and she starts to work on her decision. During this time, she gets to know a person that lives in accordance with and actively applies The Law of Possibilities. She becomes fascinated by it and discovers that many of her choices in the process of getting to where she is at now have not been by accident nor by coincidence.

Now Johanne is living in Norway and has spent her time well. She has learned to speak Norwegian and does so well. She runs her own business teaching others what the law has taught her. By applying The Law of Possibilities, she shows people that everything is possible once you know what you want and make a decision to do it.

A lot of you will think of and regard the events of Johanne's life as coincidences. According to my own and many others opinions, there is no such thing as coincidences in life. What happens is meant to happen, for whatever reason it does. The most important thing is the attitude one has toward the things that happen and how one goes about them. If you open to seeing the learning possibility in all events in life, you will gain access to a lot of development and valuable growth as a human being. It is amongst the "world of occurrences" you learn the most, because the twists of fate that The Law of Possibilities puts you in touch with usually has two facets, two sides to them, the positive or the negative. The occurrences will give you either positive or negative experiences, as the law does too, if you can see the connection here. The most important thing of all is to regard everything that happens as gifts, anyway. If you can't clearly see what's good about what has happened to you right away, you will, with a learning perspective, see the value of this as time goes by. But still, I will recommend you make use of The Law of Possibilities and decide upon what it is that are your inner dreams and wishes.

USE THE BRING-ORDER-TO-YOUR-LIFE POSSIBILITY WHEN

- it's "messy" around you,
- something challenges you more than you like,
- you know what it is you are dreaming of, but you have it all in your head,
- you have tried everything else and nothing else works,
- you want to cheer yourself up,

- you miss having someone to hold,
- you don't like the place you live,
- you need to dare to do more,
- you don't think you can do it, or,
- you think you can,
- you want to do the impossible.

What you can achieve:

You can achieve the life you want to live by being open to what life is willing to teach you, if there is something you really want.

The challenges you might face:

That you simply aren't sure of what it is you really dream of in life, or that you believe that it is unattainable. When and what kind of frequencies are you radiating?

What you specifically can do:

Start to actively undertake something.

When:

Whenever you feel ready for it and have made your mind up to do it.

There are many ways of being in touch with the law. The following story is about Lillian. She was actively applying the law, but then she got sidetracked, lost her focus, and fell back into her old habits. The story clearly tells us how important focus, energy, and awareness are to achieve your dream.

The Focus Possibility

The dream:

I Dream of Bringing More Order into My Everyday Life and in Addition, to Feel Better about Myself

Lillian came to me during a time in her life when she felt awkward and tired. She felt that she was working around the clock, both at home and at work. She always had to make things as perfect as they possibly could be and to satisfy everybody else. And the more she worked at it, the worse it got. When I met her for the very first time, her thoughts were to get through her son's confirmation, then break out of her marriage and move. What she did not realize was that she spent the majority of her time trying to find everything that was wrong with everything and everyone around her. She used The Law of Possibilities charged with negative energy and nurtured the negative frequencies so that she actually got more of the things she really did not want.

We worked out Lillian's possibility-viruses by starting to go through what it was that she did not want to have more of and then her "training camp" started. Lillian had to practice getting into a new and a more positive state of mind. One thing became very clear to her, she had lost herself somewhere along the road of wanting to satisfy everybody else—she had forgotten herself.

The possibility-viruses were the start of something new and much more exciting. She realized that she simply needed to learn to dismiss her "good girl"-attitude, or syndrome, to get more in touch with herself again. Through actively practicing every day, Lillian got back aspects of herself that she had completely forgotten she had and slowly she started to get more of what she wanted in life. Of course, there were a few humps on the road in the beginning but with each time it became easier for her to recover.

The decision to move and to start all over again turned into nothing. In line with that, Lillian found her way back to herself too. Slowly but surely it started to change. Her own radiation of positive energy was reciprocated by her husband and her children, and the truth of the law that equal attracts equal was confirmed. She wanted so much to have her man, her husband, and best friend back, and that's just what she got. They decided to spend more time together. They started to make plans for the future by taking an interest in each other's interests, they made time to go on romantic trips together and started to give one another attention in a whole new way.

Lillian learned that practice is useful and that it is a vital key to making changes in life. During this process, she also got on to a better career path, which resulted in a job offer in a big insurance company. The department she was hired in expanded quickly and so did her work demands. Slowly but surely Lillian was "consumed" by her new job and the demand to meet the expectations that it put on her. As she says: "I forgot to practice, I forgot to take care of myself and to keep focusing on my possibility-viruses." She experienced herself as a magnet for everyone with big frustrations, and she had started to drift back to the "good girl" situation in which everybody else's needs were placed before her own getting any consideration. In despair, she called me again in a cry for help. She wondered why it had to be this way.

It was easy to see what had happened. She had practiced little on her possibility-viruses. She gave her full attention to everyone around her and thus gave away all her own energy. In her eagerness to deliver in line with everyone else's expectations of her, she forgot to look after herself so that she would have energy left after a day's work.

It's good to know that Lillian is now back on track, working with and practicing on being positive with herself again. Her awareness of what it is that is important has come back to her and she's using the list of positivity-viruses on a daily basis. She's even got little reminder notes in her pockets, a technique you will read about in a later chapter. And it works. Now she is excited and happy all of the time because of how good her life is.

THE FOCUS POSSIBILITY CAN BE USED BY THOSE WHO

- want something strongly and fervently,
- have never tried the law before,
- need to practice on something,
- know how increased awareness will bring results along with it,
- want to reach far,
- want to be excited and happy about how fantastic life really is,
- have a dream of standing on their head, maybe,
- want to push boundaries for themselves,
- want to attend the school you dream of,
- want to have the place of study that you think is impossible,
- want to learn how to dance,
- have something unaccomplished.

What you can achieve:

Focus is essential; the alpha and omega when there is something you wish for. Together with increased awareness and the right attitude, you can move mountains.

The challenges you might face:

That along the way you can forget what you want to focus your attention on.

What you specifically can do:

Your possibility-viruses will be very important. You can simply decide to start employing The Law of Possibilities right now because you've become inspired.

When:

Well, what do you think?
The next story is the result of an exciting encounter. While working with this book, I wanted to get in touch with more people that had experiences with using The Law of Possibilities. I decided to send out a wish to meet a person that had dared to make changes in their life and who wished to share their story with others.
Later that afternoon, my phone rang. It turned out to be someone who wanted to sell an advertisement on a website that collected information about businesses that held classes, courses, and lectures. I told him about what I was doing and that currently my classes were put on hold. The man on the phone was very easy to talk to, and we had a very pleasant conversation about my business and

his fantastic product. Like this, the conversation swung back and forth, until I came to ask him about for how long he had been involved in his business. That's how I got the story about changes that I wished for—and even on the same day that my wish had been made!

The Change Possibility

The dream:

I Dream of Finding a New Job and to Finding the Purpose of Life Again

Just one year prior to this story, Espen worked as a store manager at a large grocery store. He had already started to get fed up with both the job and his work and duties. Espen liked to work and to be a part of things. At one time, he had held as many as three positions at once. He was a typical man of action, who forgot to get a feel for things, before one day something happened that was to start a new process within himself. The event really shook him up. At the time, Espen was living with a friend that unexpectedly ended his life. Espen was left alone and thought only of himself. The wrong focus, as he said it himself, but without understanding why. He continued his life as a man of action until his body finally one day said stop. His zest for life was completely gone. Life felt empty and it all ended with him being put on a sick leave.

To regain his strength and to get back to the joy he previously had felt, he went on a trip to a friend's cabin. He'd got only one thought in his mind and that was to completely opt out of everyday life. He started by reading a book in just 24 hours, but without even remembering what the book is about. No matter what he tried to do, happiness was completely gone from his life.

Then once more, something happened that changed his day-to-day life again, but in a positive way this time around. Espen was dragged along by his friends, almost against his own will, to watch a movie about the powers of positive thinking, about what you give of yourself is what you get in return. If it wasn't for the fact that one of these friends that dragged him along was his favorite friend, he would never have seen the movie in question. When he was asked the first time if he wanted to come along to watch it, he even refused.

But now that you are familiar with the law and know that the world is not filled with coincidences, but occurrences that have a message for you, in this case for Espen, you will understand why this movie arrived at just the right time in Espen's life and that it helped him to get back to a purpose-filled and exciting life. The message of the movie helped him to sort his mind. Then and there, he made the decision to reach for the positive and to think positive and appropriate thoughts.

Years before this happened, Espen had developed a wish to start his own business and to be part of developing something from scratch. The fact that Espen decided to think positive thoughts to change from a negative mind-set led to big changes for him in the days ahead. It took three weeks from the evening he decided to let his mind follow along positive tracks, until he was contacted and asked if he would like to be part of building and developing the company that he now works for.

The Law of Possibilities became the last part of the big puzzle that was needed for him to be able to live his life in a new way. This inconceivably simple and effective law helped turn dark and gloomy days into days filled with sunshine and happiness. What this story shows too is that you always get more of what you radiate. Espen was thinking in dark and negative ways and got more of it. Once he decided to turn around to positive thinking, progress came quickly. It can happen to you too.

> **THE CHANGE POSSIBILITY CAN BE USED BY THOSE WHO**
> - want to change their line of work,
> - get by, just ok, in mediocrity,
> - have a big dream,
> - want to do better than you are now,
> - want to develop,
> - need more courage to realize their dream,
> - are filled with creative ideas,
> - want to daydream a little,
> - want to live a more fulfilling life,
> - want to do something passionately and have their heart in it.

What you can achieve:

When you have made up your mind about something, you need to grab hold of yourself with regard to how you speak to yourself and then do something about it. If you speak in negative ways, then stop it right away! If you are positive, just keep going at it.

The challenges you might face:

That you are stuck in your old habits and that you in addition to that can't see what it takes to proceed further.

What you specifically can do:

To have an easygoing attitude, but the most important thing of all is perhaps to get back to positive thinking, regardless.

When:

How about now?
Along with this story, there's also an exciting entrepreneur possibility story. As you understand, there are no limits to the use of the law. It can be applied in many areas of life, anytime, as long as you start with the right thought.

The story about Espen brings me to the "brain" behind the business idea, to the man who developed the website for businesses involved with courses and who had seen the potential of it. The reason why I want to tell this story is that the entrepreneur possibility is also all about running a company with The Law of Possibilities as the corporate philosophy, with The Law of Possibilities as the fundamental idea and basis for leadership and motivation. It is fantastically exciting when the corporate culture builds upon the fact that equal attracts equal, which in turn is the very essence for internal motivation and external sales. It's quite possible to run and manage a company using the principles of The Law of Possibilities.

The Entrepreneur Possibility

The dream:

I Dream of Realizing My Idea of Building and Developing a Sound and Solid Business

Jens had simultaneously started three businesses and had just as much focus on all the three of them. The result was that he ran two of them adequately and the last one just ok, at least it made money. Concurrently, this creative soul had the idea of a "group of agents" within himself. As you surely understand, there was something lacking in his focus and his consciousness that The Law of Possibilities addresses. To have the same amount of focus in three different directions is quite hard, something that Jens had started to understand too.

In the same way as Espen did, it was the day that he got in touch with The Law of Possibilities that vigor came into his life.

Jens quickly got the point of the geniality of the law and inspired as he was he sat down to straighten out his businesses. The result was that he closed two of them, sold the third, and put all his energy into the idea of gathering everyone that holds lectures and courses in Norway on one website. Jens cleared his mind, "threw out" all his energy thieves, increased his awareness, and focused on what it was that really was his dream. As you can tell form the story, he focuses all his energy toward his dream. He spends some time deciding how to structure the company, what the product is supposed to be, who he wants to work with, and how big he pictures the business will be in the future. He creates a detailed and lucid wish list that's necessary to reach the dream. Jens brings together all of his positive energy, increases the frequencies, and has faith and confidence in the dream he wishes to realize, fully in line with what has to be done to make the law work.

Jens values The Law of Possibilities so greatly that he wants all the people he will be working together with to be familiar with the law and that they will make use of it. So what is more natural than to ask three of his closest friends and amongst them Espen, if they want to be part of realizing the dream. If you have experienced what the law really can bring you, it will easily become an important way of life.

What's really exciting about this story is that everyone that works together with Jens is focused on possibilities and they use the law on a day-to-day basis. The Law of Possibilities is actually a part of the human resource policy of the company and the growth they have had so far. Anybody that has any experience with sales knows that it is not always as easy to motivate yourself every day to pick the phone up to make calls to attract new customers. The difference for this company is that The Law of Possibilities has become an important tool, both for when any of the employees uses the law in a negative way or when they use it in a positive way. The difference between where they are now, after the law became a new learning experience and where they used to be, is the awareness of what it takes to consciously develop positive thinking. If one of the employees is in a state of negative frequencies, then all the others are quick on their feet to motivate positive thinking again. Now that everyone in the company knows and is familiar with the law, it usually doesn't take anything else than to remind the one that's not fluctuating the right thoughts about the contents of the law, before everything falls back in place again.

With The Law of Possibilities as a tool, the start of the business has been very successful. Their customers are positive, the results are flowing in like beads on a string, and all the drawn-up wishes, even when it comes to turnover, are where they are supposed to be.

To build a business with The Law of Possibilities as a fundamental element is fantastically exciting for the people that work there and exciting for the company's results. The law is a wonderful contribution to a positive corporate culture. Jens says that they've become so inspired by everything they've experienced so far that they are developing the business further by studying similar topics and attending courses in related fields. This has become an important part in developing the business further and one's self as a human being.

THE ENTREPRENEUR POSSIBILITY IS FOR ALL THOSE WHO WANT TO

- realize their dream,
- achieve goals,
- develop themselves together with others,
- have fun at work,
- take control of their own time,
- work with their heart in it,
- achieve success in what they do,
- live the life they want the most,
- be enthusiastic and "burn" for something, but lack courage,
- have more time to do what they really want to do.

What you can achieve:

It is possible to run a business with The Law of Possibilities as the corporate philosophy regardless of how many people are employed in the company. If it's a big or a small business doesn't really matter—it is your thoughts that count.

The challenges you might face:

This is quite innovative and you might need some time to believe that it is possible and you might have to dare to change some of your preconceptions. How about starting with yourself?

What you specifically can do:

If you think it is a good idea, then jump right in, or propose The Law of Possibilities to your boss.

When:

That's something you know best yourself.

There are many, many more similar stories and they all show that there are really no limits to which areas of life The Law of Possibilities can be applied to. We are the only ones imposing limits on ourselves.

While reading, you might have been reminded of a lot of things you have always known, that you have been in touch with and that you know that you already can do. But:

What actions have you specifically started, or which changes have you made in situations that you aren't happy with, or in which you experience that your reactions are less appropriate?

I would like to challenge you a little bit. Can you dig deep and use everything you know that you can? Can you turn it into action? Often an action can challenge you so much that you'd rather not do it or that it feels so hard to just get started. You might not really know how to begin. Maybe you wish you had someone to share your challenge with, someone that could be your supporter when you are challenged more than you think you can actually handle?

Taking Action

Now that you are familiar with the law—what can be of importance to you to know, to move on from having thoughts to taking action? My experience says that it will be vital to put the spotlight onto the act itself.

Motivation and Play

What is it that really motivates you? What is it going to take for you too to start using The Law of Possibilities? You will find lots of good answers to that question if you go back to situations and experiences you have had earlier in your life, when you really were able to achieve something you set out to do. It might just be something you did in a specific subject at school that brought you extraordinary results or other experiences that you have stored as special and valuable memories. It could be to start something that you have a burning desire to do and that you get many others to join you too. It could be skiing across the North or South Pole. It could be to become the world champion within your sport. It could be to dare to go bungee jumping. It could be to change your job. It could really be everything and anything that has led to one or another form of, in your eyes, defined success. All people have experienced one thing or another, or something they would like to call a success. Behind this experience there is a pattern, or feel free to call it strategy, if you'd like to. I call it success strategy myself, something I learned through NLP[1]. What's behind this is a specific and clearly defined approach that varies from person to person. If you have a closer look at the order of how you step by step came to achieve your perceived success, you will discover that there is a pattern in this process which repeats itself. In everything you have been successful at in life, there is a certain procedure you have followed that shows signs of similarity each time. It will be of immense importance to you to figure out this success strategy.

A strategy usually means a series of steps or milestones consciously applied toward reaching a defined goal. On the other hand, you might have to recognize that you are not always aware of what it is that has created your personal successes—what is it that you have specifically done to achieve it? A lot of the things we do happen automatically while we're on autopilot.

For you to better understand a success strategy, here I will show you an example of a purchase strategy. Let us suppose that you see (visually) a beautiful piece of art that you really would like to have. Simultaneously, you tell yourself: "Wow, that's just beautiful!" Your conversation with yourself takes you further and draws up the perspective. "Where can I put it on the wall?" Visually, the solutions come to your mind, and you experience a good feeling. You ask how much it is and think: "I can afford that" (self-conversation), and you end up deciding to buy it and you feel an extraordinary sense of happiness. This strategy can, therefore, be repeated. In the same way, you can think

---

[1] NLP stands for Neuro Linguistic Programming, which shows the relationship in between your language and the programming of your brain and body, which in turn decides your behavior.

yourself through and play with how the procedure for your success will be. The success strategy may well be called a valuable habit.

Again I will encourage and advise you to write about it. This time it will be worthwhile to start with the success and work yourself backward. Which step did you take in the part just before you reached your success? What did you do? What was the triggering factor? Analyze yourself all the way back to the point where the idea started and find your keys, which are the small steps you took along the way toward your goal. It's almost comparable to the pieces of a puzzle. If you put the pieces together, one by one, the picture will reveal itself as a beautiful image when the last piece falls into place and you can see the totality of it, "the whole picture."

There has been a whole lot of important research done around the subject of motivation. The areas that the research points out are the same as those pointed out in the success strategy mentioned above; moreover, knowing and accepting oneself seems to be one of the key concepts. In this concept lies the experience of mastering and achieving. These experiences give you belief in yourself and thus the power to be interested in something to embark on facing challenges and to be creative.

To achieve something is all about accomplishing something that has to do with being headed toward your goal, or, of course, reaching it the first time, something very few of us do. Let us take the parking possibility as an example of the law and your journey toward your goal, it being something that's the first thing you would like to try to have a go at. You put focus and energy into the thought that you will find a parking space somewhere you have decided in advance.

I assume that you do experience finding a parking space to be easier this time. Then the probability of you believing in the law will increase. The combination of the law, your thoughts, and the experience will also increase the likelihood of you even wanting to try to use the law again. Like this, you will add up your experiences and learning processes, brick by brick, one on top of another, so that the law will become something that you want to play and experiment with even further.

What's valuable to discover is that it is your inner motivation and joy of being able to master something that will be with you to encourage and motivate you even further, not the outer motivation from others. It is you who will be crucial to whether you will be motivated to act again. Practice, playing, and more practice in using the law will increase the probability of you being able to make the law work for you. It will also enhance your interest in the law, which in turn will provide you with more dividends and you will be on your way into your own valuable success strategy.

Play and have fun with the law—you don't have to take it so seriously! Lower your shoulders—it's all just fun, put a smile on your face, and have your first groundbreaking experience.

Now that you know more about the fact that the happier and more satisfied you feel, the more you follow the one you really are. And the unhappier you feel, the further you are from your own valuable source of energy. As you now know more about it, there's nothing you cannot be, do, or get. Again: what is it you want more of? You now know that if you wish to attain a natural state of happiness, you have to make the most of what you've got, and make sure you think thoughts that nurtures the state of being content. You're free and now you also know that anything that comes to you comes as a response to the thoughts you are thinking.

The Law of Possibilities is always fair. It gives you more of the thoughts you are thinking and it responds to what you send out—what you radiate. Therefore, it will be of importance for you to be aware that "equal attracts equal" and it is you who nourishes the things that come your way.

There is no such thing as a source of hardship or what you lack. Because you have the possibility to allow well-being and goodness to be yours. Consider that everything that happens to you, you have put in motion yourself. And if you don't radiate different frequencies when there's something in your life that you aren't content with, then nothing of the things you are unhappy with will change. Then your task will be to allow well-being and to work more on yourself to move beyond the resistance. Without letting go of your resistance, new personal development cannot occur.

You've been put here on earth to grow, to develop, to learn, and to have fun. I will gladly repeat: you have not been put here to struggle through life. It might provoke you to assert that you have chosen the situation you find yourself in now. But you have, consciously or unconsciously, no matter what kind of situation it is. If it is unconsciously, it might be okay to give you a wake-up call so that you can find a new approach to the situation. Or you can simply apply The Law of Possibility in a positive way so that you get closer to the life you wish for. I have a burning desire and wish for you to start making use of the law, comfortably, and to start to employ the processes that I know will change your life experiences. Let yourself be inspired by reading about others that, before you, have been able to change their situations and gotten closer to what they had set as their goal or dream. In just the same way, this is also possible for you. You will get in touch with who you really are and you will find your natural happiness—the happiness that will make each and every day adventurous and fun.

At What Time of the Day Can I Make Use of The Law of Possibilities?

The Law of Possibilities can be used anywhere and anytime. Some prefer in the morning, others before lunch, in the afternoon, or during their coffee break.

The rules of when it is possible to use the law are very generous. The law can even be applied exactly the very moment you think of it. Now, here, anytime, and anywhere.

The thoughts that bring forth your dreams can occur at any time of the day. Maybe you have to schedule an appointment with yourself or try to be less busy at where you are in life right now? Nothing's impossible—you're the boss, it is you who calls the shots and you are the one who has to make the decision. You're the one who deserves the very best of this world.

A possibility-agent will never take a break. He or she has discovered that The Law of Possibilities is much too important to grant access to all kinds of thoughts. To replenish with good thoughts that bring you good feelings will encourage the experience of good self-esteem, which is different than self-confidence. A possibility-agent knows this. In addition to that, he or she will always have it in mind to help others to become familiar with The Law of Possibilities too, so that they together will be able to live in a happier and more harmonic life.

> **DO YOU WANT TO PLAY A LITTLE BIT WITH YOUR OWN THOUGHTS?**
>
> - You have had dreams that have not yet come true. To which extent do you feel that you will be able to achieve your dreams?
> - How would it matter for your life if your dreams would come true? Which personal characteristics have brought you to where you are today?
> - Which of these personal characteristics will you increase to get you where you dream of being?
> - What would it bring you to have a life filled with happiness?
> - What is it you want? What are you really dreaming of?
> - How would it be to achieve your dream?
> - What do you have to change for your dreams to come true?
> - What are you willing to give up?
> - What are you willing to change?
> - When do you want to make these changes?
> - What do you need to be able to make the first changes?
> - Who can be your esteemed and trusted supporter along your journey of change?
> - How much love, happiness in life, and success are you willing to receive right now?

WRITE DOWN YOUR HONEST THOUGHTS HERE, OR MAKE YOUR OWN BOOK OF POSSIBILITIES!

Five Possibilities for the More Experienced

The pocket possibility
The smiling possibility
The time possibility
The refrigerator possibility
The everything-I-wish-for possibility

When you have tested The Law of Possibilities and have become familiar and comfortable with it, it might be exciting to explore some new areas in which the law can be used. That's why here you get a few playful ideas of other possibilities that you can have fun with.

The Pocket Possibility

The pocket possibility is a fun possibility. The word pocket is right because it is about what you keep in your pockets. And your pockets are only yours. It is very rare that anybody else knows what's in them. Pockets are the "bags" that are hanging in and sewn into jackets, pants, coats, and dresses, and are used to store the "this and that" you usually need to carry around with you wherever you go. The pockets could also hide your personal possibilities, possibilities that only you need to know. In other words, pockets can be used for personal development whenever you see fit.

Your pockets might not be the most familiar place for personal development, but that's even better. This possibility won't even take up that much space, either. We humans have such a nature that we, every now and then, might benefit from techniques that help us to remember valuable thoughts.

Again, I recommend writing. The pocket possibility is very effective and can be used in all pockets regardless of sizes and shapes. Use it in processes in which you want to make changes and even want to transform inappropriate behavior or for something as simple as to remember something. To make use of the powerful effects of The Law of Possibilities, it can be of value to write down what you would like to focus on, give energy and attention to, or something that you need to remind yourself of. Maybe there's a saying or a motto that you need to keep handy or connect with?

Another way of reminding yourself of those same things could be to find objects that symbolize what you want to be thinking of, like a rock or a cork. I prefer notes myself and especially in different colors.

On the note, you can write sentences of things you need to remind yourself of, like, for instance, sentences that resemble these:

- I can do anything, I have made my decision.
- Every time I make a choice, I change the future. I am choosing now.
- I am valuable.
- I have positivity within me.
- I am enjoying this moment right now.

- My health is great and I take care of it.
- I like my body.
- I give faith to everything in my life.
- I am actively applying The Law of Possibilities.
- I am always filled with possibility-viruses.
- I know I will achieve my dream.
- I am fantastic.
- I can do what I decide to do.
- I dream of ... (your dream).

Like this, you can go on indefinitely. The most important part is that what you write on your pocket possibility is something that's positively worded and in the present tense.

Now it only remains to give the note the faith it deserves. It helps to know that the note is right there in your pocket. It will give you an experience of energy. Just try it, it works! You can touch the note to experience a sense of unity and to gather energy. It might sound a little bit crazy, both to you and to others. But there are a lot of things we do that we don't share with others and everybody else does not need to know everything. Try it out. It will be amazing to discover all the possibility-viruses you might experience with a little note in your pocket.

I taught the pocket possibility to a student in high school once when she was very nervous about her English exam. She was so anxious and worried that she sat crying in a corner, when she was found by the principal. She dreaded it enormously and she had brought with her big expectations and a huge pressure to perform, both from herself and her parents, to be successful and to get a good grade. After we had talked to each other, she found a coin that she wanted to use as a symbol of her own peace and security. To ensure that she felt that she had enough knowledge and that she was well prepared. Afterward, she told me that she had touched the coin every time her anxiety had returned during the exam, and it helped her.

Maybe you too can find a symbol that will work for you.

A few weeks later, I heard that she got an "A" in her exam and that she was very satisfied with her achievement. The coin helped her to cool down her system, so that she was able to think more clearly.

Whether it's a coin or a note that you put in your pocket, you need to have your symbol with you somewhere on your body. That's of much more value than to keep it in your purse, your briefcase, or your backpack. By having your note in your pocket, you will find yourself closer to the vibrations and your chances to achieve what it is you have written on your note will increase. The biggest joy might possibly be that you discover that you are getting more in touch with The Law of Possibilities and that your faith in the law becomes strengthened.

THE POCKET POSSIBILITY CAN BE USED

- by anyone that wants to and has pockets,
- as a valuable tip for people you know or don't know, aunts, siblings, colleagues, or whomever it might be,
- to stay focused and conscious in your daily routine,
- as a reminder note for anyone with a head filled with inappropriate thoughts and nonsense,
- by all doubters who want to turn into positive believers,
- by anyone who finds purses to be in their way,

- to cheer up yourself and others,
- by those who need some help to achieve their goals and dreams,
- by those who easily forget,
- by those who are curious,
- by anyone and everyone.

Be creative. A true user of The Law of Possibilities will never let themselves be prevented from using it. Filled with possibility-viruses, this person will make use of the law everywhere and for everything. If you are a doubter, give it a chance. You don't know what you're missing out on.

What's so fabulous about The Law of Possibilities is that when you have chosen the law as your way of life, you cannot be grumpy and still smile, all at once. You have to choose either or. Now that you know that equal attracts equal, I will direct my focus toward the wonderful smile, the contagious smile, the one that does good—both for you and for everybody around you.

The Smiling Possibility

This possibility is very simple, yet exceptionally effective. It is simply all about tilting the outer edges of your lips and mouth upward and let your face glow with a big smile. You can do it right now. Try it because then, who are you really smiling at?

Very many, but first the most important person in your life—you are smiling at yourself. Feel how wonderful it is, feel how your body relaxes and enjoys it. It's hardly possible to be grouchy while you are smiling.

Positive vibrations will give you positive experiences. But you are the most important person who will benefit from the smile. To smile at yourself is like smiling inward and to add positive energies to your body, your soul, and your inner organs. Your inner landscape deserves your smile just as much as the people surrounding you.

The good thing about smiling is that you will smile both inward and outward all at once. Two birds with one stone. Because that smile will be contagious to the world, so you'd better watch out for the fact that the smile you gave to yourself, it might also actually make other people around you smile, too.

There's a little smiling story that I will happily share with you. The story is all about a coaching client that I used to work with. We had worked a lot on what smiling at others could do to him personally. In a taxi back to work after his meeting, the person involved in this story discovered what smiling at others really could lead to.

Back at work, I received a phone call from such an excited man, who told me that usually he would quietly sit in the back seat when taking a cab ride, but today he had decided to smile. The smile leads to a wish for a dialogue with the driver. He'd never had such a great cab ride ever. They'd laughed together, shared stories, and had a very nice drive. "That thing about smiling to others and to discover what I got in return has changed something in me forever," he said. A great story about smiling, and maybe an inspiration for you as a reader? Smile to the world and the world will smile back. Ever heard that one, before?

What you give of yourself will come back to you.

—Anne-Mette Røsting

> **SOME SMILING POSSIBILITIES**
> - Smiling is completely free.
> - You radiate warmth and happiness to the world.
> - You bring happiness to yourself.
> - It doesn't matter what you've got or who you are.
> - The smile is the very best virus in the world, regardless of its condition.
> - The smile can play and laugh every day.
> - You can give your smile to anyone anytime.
> - Your smile can become your trademark.
> - You will get to exercise some of the muscles in your face and that's valuable for a healthy body.
> - You will spread happiness and benevolence.
> - The smile will seal a friendship.

The one who smiles in place of showing rage is always the strongest one.

—Japanese words of wisdom

In our Western culture, we have a tradition of regarding time as passing. But why not let time be something that comes, as in African culture? We have developed a system of society where everything is based on the fact that we break time up into small units and in which the concept of time is associated with a lot of "negativity." Time is something that most people feel that they don't ever have enough of. We've created a society where everything is supposed to go as quickly as possible. Equally, we regard becoming old as something negative in our culture, whereas in other cultures age is associated with prudence and wisdom. Our perception and experience with time is linked to what we are taught as children. Turn you're thinking around and see what it will do to you: Time doesn't pass, it comes!

The Time Possibility

I don't have the time, I can't make it today, I have too much to do, some other day maybe, I don't have enough time, I have to pick the kids up from day care, I've got to catch the bus, ahhh, now I am running late again. It's just like "Karlsson-on-the-Roof" from the children's books of Astrid Lindgren so nicely puts it: "That's just an everyday thing." Is it an everyday thing for you to not have enough time and wish you had time for everything? Do you worry that you won't have enough time? Well, then you are invaded by the worry-virus. And is that really the virus you want more of? All the vibrations that are described and mentioned previously, all belong within the category of negative frequencies, and they always give you more of the same.

Words such as "don't," "too much to do," "not enough," "have to get," "got to catch" are all charged with negative frequencies that will give you more of what you radiate. It's funny how you get less and less time for those things you find pleasurable.

There's actually nothing you have to do in this world, all your "have to do's" have been chosen by you only. If you do dig deeply into a "have to do," you will find that at one point or another you chose it yourself. You said yes in a situation in which you really wanted to say, or thought, no. Consider all of the things you think you have to do. Is there something you consciously or unconsciously agree to do? How do you fill your day with tasks and assignments? Do you really have to do everything? Are all your "have to do's" a result of conscious choices?

To have enough time start with you making the decision of what it is you want to have time to do. What is it you really want to have time to do? All you need to do is to make the time to sort out all of your time thieves and to decide on what it is that's really important to you. Get a feel for it. What is it that your gut feeling says you really want to have time to do, or are there "have to do's" that are getting in your way, even if you feel that you don't want to?

Let's have a look at a very typical situation: "To be able to enjoy a nice glass of wine after work with a friend, I first have to pick the kids up from day care and then I have to go home, only to make a trip back to the city again after that. Phew, what a hassle." But do you really have to pick the kids up from day care first? Can't your better half do that? Could another friend do it for you, or could possibly a neighbor help you? Or maybe it is your conscience that's blocking you—the feeling or the frequency that you have associated with picking the kids up from day care—is that what's stopping you?

Where did you end up in this picture, and what about the nice glass of wine that would have been so pleasant to share with your friend? What is it you have to do? Nothing really. "Have to do" experiences easily occur when you say yes but really want something else.

Why don't you try to arrange yourself a little bit differently and send out possibility-viruses so that you achieve what you dream of as a pleasant way to end the day? Your child will be safe and well, and you and your friend are able to enjoy a glass of wine—yes, thank you, both please.

Say Yes to Saying No

It is very liberating to say no to something you feel that you don't want to do. The possibility-virus can give you completely unexpected, exciting experiences that you didn't think of, such as a pleasant dinner at a restaurant together with your sweetheart instead of a meeting at work that you really didn't need to attend. By saying no, people around you will become creative. "Ok, why don't we schedule the meeting for next week, because it really isn't that important, right now?"

Try it. My personal experiences were that the people around me became creative and found new solutions when I said no and meant no. I remember getting a phone call about attending a networking meeting at Lillehammer to hold a lecture. They wanted me to be there on a Friday afternoon. In the morning of that Friday, I was to start new classes as well and the roads were snowy. I would have to drive for several hours on slippery winter roads that afternoon to Lillehammer, hold my lecture, and then drive back to arrive back home around midnight, at best, instead of spending my Friday evening together with my family. I thought about it and said no thanks. Then, the lady on the other end of the phone suddenly asked me if she could call me the following week. That week, the same lady called and asked me if I would rather hold the lecture at the networking meeting they would have in Oslo in spring. Then, it was easy to say yes. I learned something valuable that a no also can inspire creativity and that the end result could be even better.

This story taught me a valuable lesson in saying no. I went from being a yes person to a person who listened to how I felt about the situation, if it felt right at for that moment I could choose which suited me best.

To say no because you really mean it, is incredibly powerful. And by all means make sure you put away the thought that it's all about selfishness.

Selfishness and egoism are colloquially often used as synonyms of ruthless, reckless, and irrational behavior. But that's not how it is in reality. Be aware of the fact that you are only behaving like your own true self when you get a feel for and make choices, based on what it is that you need and wish for. All people are individuals; there aren't two who are completely alike. All individuals have their own special wishes and needs and that's quite alright.

You are unique and you are the most important person in your life. Egoism is just a negatively charged word, which all pessimistic souls believe in and use, without perhaps being very conscious about it. It is not an act of egoism to take care of and to respect one self. The definition of the term egoist is to act on your own behalf. That's the same as being useful to yourself and so that your actions benefit yourself. It's in the nature of things that nobody can live without having benefit from their own actions. That's why egoism is the ethics of life. Ethics are all about values, and values cannot exist without life.

Say YES to saying NO and dare to be all of yourself, then you will always find the time to do the things you want to do.

> **THE TIME POSSIBILITY IS EXCELLENT FOR**
> - those who are always in a hurry,
> - those who dream of the mountains,
> - those of you who need to have more appropriate thoughts,
> - all stressed-out normal people who want changes,
> - those who fully enjoy life and need some encouragement,
> - those of you living by the clock,
> - those of you that don't know that time is something that will come to you.

The time possibility is loving and tender, filled with happiness, and is contagious, wonderful, and including but the best part of all: it is yours. The possibility is yours, the choice is yours, because after all you are the boss of your own life.

> *One half of the world cannot understand the pleasures of the other.*
>
> —Jane Austen

Every possible surface can be used to disperse possibilities: the mirror in the bathroom, the hallway, the living room, the door to your room, the door of your office, the basement, the rest room, your computer screen, your mobile phone, and your desk—even the door of your refrigerator. Just have a look at this:

The Refrigerator Possibility

The law can be applied everywhere and always. It is just your imagination that is the limit. In this story, The Law of Possibilities is written on a note. The note could be hung from a funny magnet on your refrigerator door, as long as it is a message that you would like to share with others.

At our house, the refrigerator door is often used as a message board for notes and other cheerful greetings. Others might use this space to put up pictures, greeting cards, or even bills. Here, I will give you another idea of how you can make use of the refrigerator door.

It was winter, it was a Sunday and the youngest one in our family was to participate in a skiing competition. He was actively involved in downhill skiing, and this was the time of the year for competing. Saturdays and Sundays were usually spent on a ski slope somewhere. This Sunday we were in Lommedalen, in the suburbs of Oslo, Norway. For a while, there had been a note on the fridge that said: "You can do anything, you just have to make the decision." The words of that note were neatly framed, with gold stars glued around them. Visually, it was a note that was easy on the eyes and quite obviously our youngest one has glanced at it several times without us knowing anything about it.

On this particular Sunday, our youngest one was about to reveal a whole new side of himself. Right from the start, he ran the course faster than we had ever seen him run before. The time displayed on the scoreboard showed that he had made a fast run, too. A great result that ranked him very high on the list of results. I think he must have been just nine or ten years old.

I just couldn't help it, I just had to ask: "What was it that actually happened to you today, sweetie? I don't think

I have ever seen you ski this fast?" His words brought me to think of what the note on the refrigerator door had done to him. He just looked up at me with his beautiful blue eyes and with a huge and proud smile, he said: "Mom, I just did what it says on the note."

Something as small as a note on the refrigerator door resulted in such a huge achievement. He made use of The Law of Possibilities unconsciously that time, created the dream of going as fast as he could, increased the frequencies, and allowed it to happen. The result did not go amiss, or unnoticed.

The Everything-I-wish-for Possibility

You can achieve absolutely anything you wish for.

Ok, stop for a second. What did you think when you read that sentence? What was it that entered your mind and your thoughts just now? Was it a positive or a negative frequency? Were you invaded by a possibility-virus or was it a worry-virus that popped up to say: "Hey, here I am!" For your sake, I hope it was the possibility-virus. You should also know that it isn't always the possibility-virus that arrives at first. The most important thing of all is that you discover which virus it is that's about to contaminate your body. If it is the possibility-virus, then you should simply lean back, enjoy, and receive it—you should even be as greedy as possible and take with you as much of it as possible. Take it with you for all it is worth. Wish all the possibility-viruses a heartily welcome and make sure they arrive in such large quantities that they are a challenge to receive all at once. Smile, enjoy, and be there with your whole self.

On the other hand, if it is the worry-virus that shows up and you recognize it, you should also be happy and proud, too. That will tell you that you have increased your consciousness and your awareness and made yourself able to tell that there's something unwanted around and that you can stop those thoughts. The word "stop" can be very useful when the worry-viruses are trying to get onto the field. It is a word that I myself find to be of great value when my thoughts drift off in the wrong direction, and it is very effective. It is also a very good starting point from which you can figure out what it is you want more of. You'll never be able to express more concisely what it is you want more of, until you discover something you don't want. Stop, flick the switch over, and think about what it is that's important for you to focus on now. At the very same instant the negative frequency ceases and the positive radiation will start to work on you. Immediately, you'll be back on track, back on the train that will take you where you want to be. It is so much more exciting to start out with thoughts that will bring good and positive results.

Consider this: it is impossible to be in positive and negative frequencies all at once, so make sure you choose the positive ones. "Always look on the bright side of life."

WHAT WILL GET YOU INTO POSITIVE FREQUENCIES?

Feel free to use sentences such as:

- I have decided to ...
- A lot can happen ...

How quickly The Law of Possibilities will work for you will be directly proportional with how much of it you allow.

The Everything-I-wish-for Possibility is For Everyone—Always

You don't have to save the entire world. Save yourself. Make sure that you are happy. That means that you have to focus on those things that make you thrive and prosper, the things that make you happy and what makes you experience what you want is headed in your direction, the things that give you the experience of success.

Go easier in life. Like most others, you may take life a bit too seriously. The meaning of life is that we are supposed to enjoy it and have fun, right? You have come here to this earth, to live, to rejoice in everything that happens. Always be thankful of yourself, proud of yourself, and happy with the fact that you are just who you are and nobody else.

You are born into this life as someone unique. There is nobody quite like you. Be kind to yourself, and be the original edition of yourself that you were meant to be, or take back the original you, that you know you really are, if you have taken a wrong turn because you consider others more important than yourself. It is always better to be a charming original rather than a poor copy.

You can become blind by seeing each day as a similar one. Each day is a different one, each day brings a miracle of its own. It's just a matter of paying attention to this miracle.

Everyone seems to have a clear idea of how other people should lead their lives, but none about his or her own.

—Paulo Coelho

To be a Little Bit Crazy is to be Normal

But not in the eyes of the masses. Mediocrity despises success above anything on earth. Know that when you achieve your goal and your dream, others around you might attack you. Maybe you already have experienced it. They feel awkward and uncomfortable. People are often only satisfied when you are at the same level as them. If you go a level higher than theirs, they become distressed, feel bothered, and are discontented with themselves. Know that they are lacking your courage and that it is too painful for them.

Work on moving beyond a sense of competition, even though you live in a society in which competition is an important part of life. At least make sure that the only person you are competing with is yourself.

"I wish it was me" is not a positive feeling filled with good energy. No, then it will be better to celebrate. Remember to celebrate every time you or someone else achieves something. Make sure you celebrate others just as much as you would celebrate yourself. If you employ your enthusiasm, you will only get even more of it. Great!

Bring out your magic wand as often as you can— radiate enthusiasm, jump with joy, fling your arms out, celebrate everything that can be celebrated, smile your most beautiful smile as often you can, and share your most infectious laughter. Let loose all of these fantastic viruses you have within yourself, set them free and make your life an arena for the fantastic joy that will help you to feel as if every single day of your life is like a party, if you want to. Celebration is real, valuable, and enriching thankfulness.

Say, think, feel, and be happy because "Happiness will bring happiness along with it," as Bjørnstjerne Bjørnson, who wrote the lyrics of the Norwegian national anthem, so beautifully formulated it. That's how easy it is. The one that makes it hard, if you think it is hard to find happiness, is no one other than yourself. It is only you and nobody else who is responsible for your own life. It is your thought that holds the key to all changes in your life.

If you want to experience more success in life, then the first and foremost indicator of this is how much happiness you feel. The really happy and joyful people are those who can sense genuine happiness, are eager to move on, and who want to share their cheerfulness with themselves and with others.

Success is all about joyful moments, and a joyful life is just a long series of joyful moments. For that reason, it is all about allowing happiness instead of being too busy trying to create an enjoyable life full of things rather than happiness. You don't really need to own a thing, or earn money, to find happiness. All you need to do is to allow happiness to be.

The only thing you need to do is to decide what it is you want in life and then open up and allow it to receive it. Yes, you can.

To be a little bit "crazy" is to be normal but not in the eyes of the masses. Most people are just standing around, preferring you to be just like them. They cannot accept the thought that you have achieved something they themselves missed out on. You have to gather courage and know that if someone thinks you are crazy, enjoy that thought. There is actually room for a lot of wonderful, crazy people and all the great people of our world have been a little bit crazy in the eyes of the masses.

The best thing for you to do will always be to continue along your path toward your own dream and to think positive, appropriate thoughts to yourself. Never let go of your focus on that one day you will achieve your dream. When you have allowed yourself to follow the path you need to go—when you have practiced reaching your goal—when you feel that you have crossed the finish line, you will experience success and become a hero in the eyes of the masses. So what do you want to be: just another copy of the masses, or a crazy hero? The choice is yours.

From success you get a lot of things,
but not that great inside thing that love brings you.
—Samuel Goldwyn

RADIATE ALL YOUR UNLIMITED, POSITIVE ENERGY NOW, SO THAT

- the media can put more focus on the positive and valuable things that happen every day,
- more people will see the true beauty of the world,
- more people can share their thankfulness, instead of just thinking about it,
- more people can start using the words "I'm sorry,"
- more people can give each other encouraging and flattering words along on their path of life,
- more than just friends and family will remember your birthday,
- we together can create movements toward something and not just movements against something,
- everyone who has challenges can be better through positive, mental training,

- more people can increase their awareness of the fact that most worries never amount to anything and that they are only temporary,
- more people can share their beautiful smile with each other on a day-to-day basis,
- more people will think that time is something that comes and that you do have more than enough of it,
- more people could use both halves of their brain equally and just as much so that there would be a better balance throughout the world,
- all the children and the youth of the world will gain access to the help they need to create a secure future for themselves,
- we all put in our best effort to reduce the environmental emissions and that together we start taking better care of our earth,
- everyone in the world will have what they need to be happy people,
- more people will come to peace with themselves,
- everyone can unite for peace, not war,
- you can be thankful and sense thankfulness every day,
- you too can choose life in the light,
- so that we together can make the world a better place.

What if You Already Are Happy?

Then, everything will be quite alright. There is nothing you need, there's nothing that has to change. To be in this situation is all about being at terms with yourself and to be in touch with your own energy, not just your physical strength. To be at terms with yourself is that there is coherence in between the thoughts you think, how you feel, and what you radiate. When you're at terms with yourself, when you are in touch with your fantastic potential, you feel whole and complete. Then, it won't matter to you which table you are seated at in a restaurant, how huge the traffic jam is, how the stock market develops, what you wear, or what you own. The reason for why you let yourself become affected by situations like these is that you let your surroundings and your environments influence you. "If I'd just gotten that table by the window, then I would have been happy." "If the traffic hadn't been so bad I'd gotten there faster and then I would have been happy." "If I'd only lived in a mansion, then I would have been happier."

One of the paths to discover that everything is ok is to actively use The Law of Possibilities, think positive thoughts, see the possibilities, and to find your path into the good feeling.

The power of the mind is incredibly strong. It is the power of your thinking that determines whether you are able to be yourself fully and completely, which is one of the highest states of fulfillment you can ever attain, and that has to be what all people, in their inner most dreams, want to achieve. Coincidentally, you should also know that it is very easy to say: "I'm just being myself and you'll have to take me as I am." But think this one through. Are you really being yourself, or is this just something you are saying to put your guard up and to protect yourself against the world around you?

The process of being yourself, fully and completely, starts with you accepting everything you are, what you have been, and who you will become. Not being yourself usually originates from some kind of fear. What are you scared of? Because, if you are to accept yourself and to be able to attain happiness, you have to start by letting go of your fears, so that you can find peace. It is only then you can really be yourself. To free yourself from fear, you will have to move yourself away from that large serving of common fears that exist within a lot of people. You have to move yourself toward freedom. But that takes courage that will help you to start to be your own true self, so that you can find your inner peace. In this state of mind, you will also get a feel for the balance in between the two halves of the brain. And love will emerge as a wonderful feeling, as a consequence and a result of the thoughts that balances it all. Yes, you have a choice, and yes, you can do it.

> *Happiness is when what you think, what you say, and what you do are in harmony.*
>
> —Mahatma Gandhi

The Face of Love

The real key to being your own true self is to know what's in your own heart, so that you dare to be all of yourself. When you as a human being are hindered from following your heart—what you feel that you wish to be or to do, you become reduced. You hand away your own judgment, and you might possibly even hold yourself back. The opposite is to be encouraged by your cheerleading squad and yourself to be yourself, so that you develop a whole lot of wonderful wisdom, understanding, and happiness. To follow your heart will also be the same as to be all of yourself to others, which in turn is exactly the same as equal attracts equal. That you know your heart makes you who you are. The more and the better you become familiar with yourself and who you are, the more other people will too. They'll be more able to see the beauty within you and will be drawn towards you.

This condition can be perceived as difficult, or even outright impossible for a lot of people who are a part of the world we live in. Today, in our part of the world, people experience peace. We live longer, we are consistently and all in all healthier, and we enjoy the freedom and the prosperity we are a part of. This is due to the increased prosperity of the last century. Nevertheless, there are lots of us still searching for happiness without being able to find it. In earlier times, happiness was not a topic. Then, it was all about surviving, to cover the basic needs of food and warmth.

Today, most of us in the Western part of the world have our basic needs covered easily, which gives us a lot of time to think of other things we want. It is a natural thing for us humans to strive for status, and we have developed a culture which is all about "more," "better," and "best." That's why we are constantly looking out for more material prosperity, more security, and more happiness. Still, people are less happy and less secure now than they were 50 years ago. Along with the status we have accomplished and are enjoying nowadays, a new level of anxiety has also entered our lives: the more you hunt and strive for status and belongings, the greater the likelihood will be for you to develop a fear of being without it. Again this often leads to you spending less time developing yourself, which in turn takes you further and further away from your own true self. In this fervor, you are always on the lookout for more things that will contribute to your perceived sense of happiness—a vacation, a new car, more education, or a new relationship. You cry out loud and may even envy those who have everything that you are dreaming of. The only thing that happens is that you become trapped by your own problems. It is easier to lose yourself now than ever before.

So where are you to find the happiness you are looking for? Happiness comes from focus and awareness within yourself—there, within yourself, is where you will find the answers to everything you are dreaming of. A heart bursting at its seams with positive possibility-viruses will always guide you towards happiness. As soon as your fears are healed, happiness will become present. Once you have healed your fears, you will understand that happiness is exactly where you are now, today, nowhere else externally, no other place besides within yourself. The kind of happiness I am talking about will last forever—regardless of whether you are having a good day or a difficult day, if you accomplish what you are dreaming of or if you are struggling to make it. Whether in your eyes something is right or wrong, you will be at one with happiness because it is you, within you, and with you. Everything is about you and your relationship with yourself, not in everything that goes on in the outer world. You were born to be happy. Learn to enjoy the moment and life as it is now. If you understand what happiness is, you will always look for the possibilities and what it is you need to change when facing something that challenges you. In the end, happiness is a personal choice. Happiness depends on how you see the world and your own part in it.

If you're not aware of your purpose in life then don't worry. Just live this life because that's how you give life its purpose and meaning. It isn't important to know the meaning of life to be able to live it. Life brings with it its own concealed powers that you will only discover by living it.

When you use The Law of Possibilities with your heart, sense it and keep your focus and awareness on happiness, the use of the law will lead to success. And the secret behind any success is to discover that you accept life fully and completely and what life brings to you, each and every day.

Love is a fruit in season at all times and within reach of every hand.

—Mother Teresa

The Law of Possibilities is so Simple, Habits Make it Complicated

The law is supposed to be simple and easy to use. The reason why you might experience the law as complicated is within yourself, your thoughts, and what you think is possible. Everything is possible as long as you have enough belief in that you can achieve your goals. Think through how you normally are affected by the world around you, or if you are capable of putting into practice what you believe in yourself. Here is an important key to succeed with the law. The value of the law will increase for you as you go along, if you try it, test it, focus, and increase your awareness. Everything is between your ears, in the form of thoughts and feeling, and how much you are willing to practice.

It is all about trying, maybe even failing at it every once in a while, but then making it, experiencing success, developing, and growing. Self-discipline will also be an important factor.

Don't make it complicated. Think simple thoughts, do simple actions, and make life into something positive and straightforward. Could it be easier? Go beyond the negative thoughts and the skepticism you might feel and you will only end up with receiving more of it. The Law of Possibilities will always give you more of what it is you are asking for.

> *Knowledge is proud that it knows so much, wisdom is humble that it knows no more.*
>
> *—William Cowper*

Make the Time

As I emphasized in the time possibility, we live in a society where everything has to go fast and faster and faster. We don't have time, we are always rushed, we don't have enough time, we have to hurry, we have to apologize for being late or that we will be delayed, we simply can't make it. And just like this, the days and the lives of a lot of people go on. Now that you know the law, you also know why a lot of people are trapped in this situation. These people simply give nourishment to all the things they don't have time for and just get more of the same. Another paradox is that now, because the technological developments are so quick, there are more and more products that are supposed to help you with time management, but yet you still experience that time does not suffice. Something must be wrong somewhere. The Law of Possibilities is all about taking your time back, to give yourself time, to achieve results quickly or over time, to enjoy progress, and then move on.

The most important part is that whatever you devote your time to also gives you something valuable in return. That goes for The Law of Possibilities too.

> *There are no shortcuts to any place worth going.*
>
> —Beverly Sills

So you will also know that a year or two is not a long time if that's the time you need to get to where you want to be.

More people will enjoy setting some time aside to actually live their lives and not just rush along, so that they miss all the possibilities along the way. Stop for a little while and gather what you need, and then go on.

> *The cycle of life is the same whether you conduct it smiling or crying.*
>
> —Japanese words of wisdom

In a similar way, the positive frequencies of The Law of Possibilities will be there for you if you decide to make use of them.

Why Is This Book for You?

Because I believe that if more people are engaged in positive thinking and keep their focus on the fact that anything is possible, that everything can be done, that I can do it, that I will put in my very best effort and be satisfied, then more people will be able to attain a greater peace with themselves. By focusing on possibilities, more dreams can come true.

We can reduce the number of wars and violence in this world if we are focused on peace. We'll find it easier to accept one another, we will respect each other's religious beliefs, we will open up to view our fellow human beings as they are, respect them, accept them, be responsible for ourselves, and move on in life without even casting a glance to the side and wonder about what others may think of it. In this way, you will be able to reach your full potential, be all of yourself, and enjoy both your own and others' successes equally. If you are at peace with yourself, we're one step closer to achieving peace for the world, and we can live in a world in which everyone feels better about themselves. I still believe that all people are basically good people, and that everyone has an inner wish to be good to others.

With these last words, I will send you off on your own into the exciting life you have laying in front of you waiting to be used, waiting for you to increase your awareness of what your dreams are, and waiting for you to focus on applying The Law of Possibilities every day to achieve your dreams—the law of equal attracts equal. Yes, you can do it.

You can do anything, you just have to make the decision to do it. Your life is yours, and only yours, and it is also only you who can make the choices of how you want to be challenged and how you want to live your life.

Have you filled your life with your past, and you are walking around carrying old baggage, that additionally even feels heavy to carry? That just makes life unnecessarily hard. Get rid of the things you don't need anymore. Life is "now," your past was a moment ago or yesterday. Your past is already history, and you don't need to bring all of it with you on your journey further into the life ahead of you. The past has admittedly brought you where you are now. Be thankful for the gifts you have received, which can be found in the learning experiences you have had. Bring with you just those things you really need and continue forward and ahead.

Your power is in the "now." The only reality we have is "now." What we do and how we spend every moment is what creates our destiny. The only thing that can stand in the way of our reality of "now" are two things within us that holds our energies back: the past and the future. Everything that has happened to you is just thoughts you have stored in your memory: your reality is all about your personal experiences. That's why the past is no longer a reality, it's gone forever. It's an illusion, so just let it disappear.

You have not yet created your future with your thoughts, your feelings, your words, and actions, and that's why your future is not a reality either. Let your worries and your fears about the future vanish and fade away. Both your past and your future are illusions at the moment.

The Law of Possibilities is valuable when you are creating positive dreams because then you have the possibility to lay the foundation for positive actions. The Law of Possibilities will help you to realize your dreams and simultaneously provide you with the experience of joy and happiness in what is "now." Yes, you can do it.

> *Do not be afraid to progress forward slowly, but do be afraid of standing still.*
>
> —Chinese proverb

There are no limitations whatsoever in this world. The limitations only exist in your mind, in your thoughts about what's possible. When you open up to the unlimited creative energies that abounds, you will be able to receive a whole new world. Right now, you are standing at the threshold of an awesome possibility, the possibility of a new beginning, the possibility to create a future that's filled with all of the joy, and the happiness you are wishing for. You can create it now.

It has taken me many years to reach where I am now—to reach that state in my life where I can live consciously and focus on seeing all of the possibilities that exist to live every day in happiness. It was the day when I finally understood that finding happiness in life solely relied on my own thoughts that my life really took a new turn. That reason precisely is why I so eagerly want to share The Law of Possibility with you so that you too can experience the same as I did. Whether you're young or old doesn't matter. You can start at any point in life. The most important thing is that you start. Just like one of Norway's most known authors so beautifully expressed it on her 90th birthday, "Old age is not just a waiting room for the termination of life. There's so much to fill your days with. I've just bought a new bed, I still write every day, I read, and I rejoice in the present day."

Have fun, laugh, and happily work with The Law of Possibilities every day. Now that you are familiar with the law and that you have met exciting people who have shared their fantastic stories with you, what are you waiting for?

Nothing is impossible, absolutely nothing. What can make a difference is The Law of Possibilities—a natural part of your potential, your fantastic inner strength, a combination of your thoughts, feelings, words, and actions which you can put to use right now. "Now." And regardless of how you choose to apply The Law of Possibilities, it will be what's right for you!

I wish you, with all of my heart, fantastic experiences with The Law of Possibilities. As a possibility-agent, you will be filled to the brim with possibility-viruses in a world filled with possibilities, what you are a part of. Think, live, and do as if you already have had your dreams fulfilled. Be a bit more like children are, see past your obstacles.

There will always be several roads leading to Rome—your path is the only one that's right for you.

Get ready. Have faith and enjoy the good, joyful, and inspiring journey you are about to embark on. Yes, you can do it!

You must be the change you want to see in the world.
—Mahatma Gandhi

A Short Summary of The Law of Possibilities

> **WHAT YOU GIVE FOCUS, ENERGY, AND ATTENTION TO BECOMES A REALITY WHETHER IT IS WANTED OR UNWANTED**
>
> Step 1 Define your dream
> Step 2 Increase the frequencies—believe it is possible
> Step 3 Allow it to happen

Recommended Tools

A sheet of paper that you divide in half with a line along the middle—one half for your worry-viruses and one half for your possibility-viruses. A pen and crayons too, if you prefer colors. Or, maybe a computer, you can use either?

Extras

A glass filled with something good to drink, candles, soft background music, and the mobile phone turned off.

Start

If it feels hard to get started, why don't you start by writing down the things you are not satisfied with in your life right now, so that your consciousness is awakened. Find your worry-viruses, or start by making a list of your dreams and goals written in the present tense, which will be your possibility-viruses.

The Next Step

Go into your heart, feel, and search for a connection between your thoughts and your feelings.

Accessories

A huge smile, your creativity, a good-sized helping of curiosity, and your own happiness.

To be Able to Achieve Results

Spend time "practicing," "practicing," and "practicing."

When Things Start to Happen

Enjoy it all and make sure you celebrate yourself a lot, jump up and down, dance, and be happy.

An Invitation, a Request, and an Encouragement

Be at one with The Law of Possibilities, and share it with as many as possible.

Goal

Become an actively practicing possibility-agent, contaminating as many as possible with possibility-viruses.

Did You Say Difficult?

Turn on the positive frequencies then or have a peek at feedback from other readers for more inspiration.

In positive psychology, one is focused on that people are born with lots of talents and skills that are available to them and it is vital that they discover them. With The Law of Possibilities, you really have gained access to a tool to unlock and get closer to your own potential. But, do be patient with yourself. As the psychologist William James once said: "It is in the winter we learn to swim and it is in the summer we learn to ski." Put in another way: your new experiences must be allowed to sink in. You must allow for practice and let your new experiences become a part of you.

There's nothing you cannot be, do, or get in your life. And you are the boss. It is only you that can convince yourself about the truth you want to see in your life.

The Aha Experience

What I want for you with this book is that you now have had a huge aha experience because there is a very simple, user-friendly law that you can carry out and live with. A law that also at the same time has given meaning and clarity to experiences you have had before, that you until now have called coincidences, for better or for worse.

> **THIS BOOK IS DIFFERENT BECAUSE**
>
> You can make changes in your life that will make a difference to you.
>
> Not because of me writing this for you, but a difference because of yourself.

- There will not be any changes if you are waiting for your surroundings or on others.
- You are solely the change you are longing for.
- You are your own hope for the future.
- You can change.
- You can act.
- You can start "now."
- You can make a difference for yourself.
- You can.
- Yes, you can do it!

The Institute of Possibility-thinking

> **Membership Card**
>
> It is confirmed that ………………………………… (your name) has decided to become an actively practicing possibility-agent and has devoted his or her life to share the possibility-virus with as many people as possible on a national and international basis.
>
> ……………………………………………
>
> The Possibility Thinking Department (sign.)

THINK POSSIBILITES—BE POSSIBILITIES—
CREATE POSSIBILITIES AND SEE
POSSIBILITIES—EVERY DAY
YES, YOU CAN DO IT!

I have made my decision:

……………………………………………

Signature
Diagnose: Do you wonder what you
will be when you "grow up?"
Treatment: Introduce The Law of Possibilities.
Prognosis: Very, very good.

A Bit about Everything

Do You Want to Get in Touch with Other Possibility-agents?

In that case, go to the Facebook page: Law of Possibilities.

More can be done to break down the cultural and emotional barriers that hold you back from experiencing the strengthening and developing experience that The Law of Possibilities can bring to your life.

My Facebook page is a playful and loving contribution to you and all other curious souls who wish to bring out their full potential and who want to reach the dream they have.

To become a member of www.facebook.com/Law-of-Possibilities is easy. Believe that The Law of Possibilities is active and make up your mind! Decide to become an actively practicing possibility-agent and sign the membership card which confirms that you have decided to give energy, focus, and attention to a positive use of the law. Tell others about The Law of Possibilities, and share positive possibility-viruses with the rest of the world. See if you can make more people discover this fantastic law and invite them along on your "journey" to the possibilities of progress and good health. Share the message wherever you are in the world. You can do it and of course you'll make that decision.

Let The Law of Possibilities become your new way of life and not something you resort to every now and then. Use it everywhere and always. It is my hope that The Law of Possibilities will become an everyday thing, a fantastic way of living that will give you more of what you want and less of what you don't want.

As a member, you will be able to take part in the experiences of others and simultaneously share your own. You will be able to ask questions and get answers, you will meet people who are interested in the same things as you, namely to see the possibilities of the world.

Go to www.facebook.com and "Law of Possibilities."

It is a Facebook society that will be created by you as a user. There's just one requirement to make you an active user of the society and to gain access to the page and that's that you have made the decision to use The Law of Possibilities. The page is not a discussion site where there's room for negative thinking. The page is exclusively a positive possibility page for those of you who have decided to follow The Law of Possibilities. It is for those of you who want to have so much of an experience with the law what you discover the fantastic feeling of being an actively practicing possibility-agent with the aim of wanting to share possibility-viruses.

SOURCES OF INSPIRATION

Books

The Alchemist by Paulo Coelho. Harper Torch, 1998.
End the Struggle and Dance with Life by Susan Jeffers. St. Martin's Griffin, 1997.
The Hug Therapy Book by Kathleen Keating. Hazelden, 1995.
The Power of Now by Eckhart Tolle. New World Library, 2004.
Ask and It Is Given by Ester Hicks and Jerry Hicks. Hay House, 2005.
Law of Attraction by Michael J. Losier. Wellness Center, 2007.
Stars and Planets by Ian Ridpath. Princeton University Press, 2008.
Tankestreker by Knut M. Nesse. Arneberg Forlag, 2000 (Norwegian).
The Aladdin Factor by Jack Canfield and Mark Victor Hansen. Berkley Books, 1995.
The Light Shall Set You Free by Dr N. Milanovich and Dr S. McCune. Athena Publishing, 2005.
The Secret by Rhonda Byrne. Atria Books, 2006.
The 7 Habits of Highly Effective People by Stephen R. Covey. Free Press, 2004.
The Tibetan Art of Living by Christopher Hansard. Atria Books, 2003.
The Tibetan Art of Positive Thinking by Christopher Hansard. Atria Books, 2005.
The Tibetan Art of Serenity by Christopher Hansard. Pegasus Books, 2007.
Lyrics from Monty Python, written by Eric Idle.

About the Author

Anne-Mette Røsting is an intuitive visionary, philanthropist, and a changemaker. With a Masters of Business Administration degree, specializing in marketing and organizational management, she has over 15 years of experience in managing large international companies and mentoring at the Norwegian Business School. She is also a trained practitioner of neuro-linguistic programming (NLP), a technique that focuses on language and the processes that determine our behavior. Anne-Mette has been running her own consultancy, Natural Force, for the past 22 years, through which she coaches and provides guidance to business organizations. Her lecture "You always get what you ask for," inspired by the thoughts surrounding the law of attraction, is very popular. It focuses on positive thinking and on how to understand and make use of the great resources that everyone has within them.

Anne-Mette is enthusiastic, committed, and ardently involved in what she does. An experienced public speaker, she is vibrant on stage and gets everyone, from all levels of business, to enjoy themselves. Anne-Mette also presents tailor-made lectures and courses on "change," "communication," and "joy of life." Her book *The Law of Possibilities* is a best seller in Norway and has helped many people achieve their goals.

For all motivational speaking appearances, please contact post@naturalforce.no

For more information please visit www.naturalforce.no

LinkedIn Search: Anne-Mette Røsting

Facebook: www.facebook.com/Law of Possibilities

Instagram: annemetterosting

Twitter: @mulighetsloven

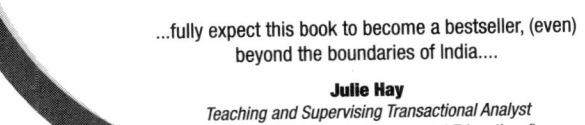

...fully expect this book to become a bestseller, (even) beyond the boundaries of India....

Julie Hay
Teaching and Supervising Transactional Analyst (Organizational, Psychotherapy, and Educational)

Enhance Your People Skills

For special offers on this and other books from SAGE, write to marketing@sagepub.in

Explore our range at
www.sagepub.in

₹395

Paperback
978-93-866-0200-8

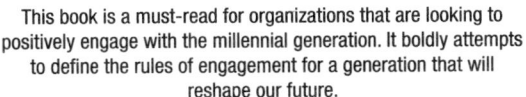

This book is a must-read for organizations that are looking to positively engage with the millennial generation. It boldly attempts to define the rules of engagement for a generation that will reshape our future.

Kiran Mazumdar-Shaw
Chairperson and Managing Director, Biocon

A Fascinating Eye-Opener into the Life of Y!

For special offers on this and other books from SAGE, write to marketing@sagepub.in

Explore our range at www.sagepub.in

₹495

Paperback
978-93-866-0274-9

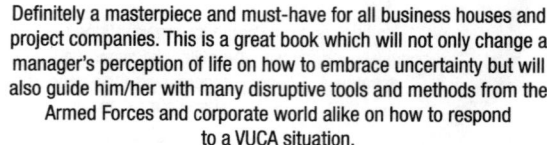

> Definitely a masterpiece and must-have for all business houses and project companies. This is a great book which will not only change a manager's perception of life on how to embrace uncertainty but will also guide him/her with many disruptive tools and methods from the Armed Forces and corporate world alike on how to respond to a VUCA situation.
>
> **Tapan Misra**
> Director, Space Applications Centre, ISRO, Ahmedabad

Master the Art of Dealing with VUCA the Armed Forces Way!

For special offers on this and other books from SAGE, write to marketing@sagepub.in

Explore our range at
www.sagepub.in

₹450

Paperback
978-93-866-0231-2